The Unchained mind

Before we get started I underlined some very important points I never want you to forget. Please enjoy

CHAPTER ONE

Sampson was a below-average kid by most people's standards. He was below average or "special" as he lacked the attention span to concentrate on any one thing for too long. He was born black and poor in the rural south. He was free, but that was just a word because there was no real freedom by any means. There were opportunities for free blacks, but most did not qualify for these opportunities because most could neither read nor write. So, for most, this almost guaranteed that they would continue working the same jobs they worked as slaves. They never learned to count, so they remained at the mercy of the farm owners, who cheated them out of their pay and anything else they could get away with. Because of this inflicted disadvantage, they cheated and mistreated the free slaves regularly. Sampson was good with his hands. He learned mostly from watching others but also had a gift for creating out-of-the-box ideas from scrap parts and broken tools he found lying around.

Little Sampson was sent from farm to farm as a cleaner of sorts. He could organize a cluttered shed in an evening. By the time Sampson finished, everything would be straight and placed in its designated space before the day's end. In the end, Sampson could tell you the location of every piece of equipment as he was excellent at organizing things and knowing exactly where everything was located, irrespective of the job size. Little Sampson could keep any parts that the farmers didn't want; this gave him a mass of parts to choose from to aid him in creating his inventions. He was good at envisioning things in a way that the average person didn't.

Although this may sound like some glorious gift, I can tell you that until this point, it does not seem to amount to anything at all. After all, look at the surroundings he finds himself in. You can call his life anything but special.

Even though he could not learn like the others, he was intelligent in ways not even apparent to him. But I think as time goes on, he is going to find out just how extraordinary he really is. You would think life as a free slave was better, but for most, it didn't change. Actually, in reality, mostly, things remained the same as before. The society that the slave was accustomed to was not designed to accommodate their freedom. So this so-called free society remained levied against them almost the same as it was from the beginning. Even if they had some sense of being free, their existence and earnings were still low compared to their white counterparts. So the insinuation of a term like freedom to a slave felt like nothing more than a useless name that accompanied their oppression. Or maybe it was just a prettier name they felt would satiate the dissatisfaction that the slaves felt as they fought for and yearned to be free. After all, if you were inferior from the beginning and were as frequently as practicably reminded, you would eventually become accustomed to thinking this way. You would accept what they gave you and not feel important enough to ask for or think you deserved more.

Being slaves who never learned how to read created a vastly different living experience for the whites and former slaves. The younger freed slaves were told by the older generation that they used to be kings and rulers. The old would tell the young of vast amounts of land they owned and the freedom they had in their homeland. Most of the young who heard this thought it was a fairytale. They couldn't relate to the stories because the stories neither explain their living standard nor could it explain how they wound up in such a predicament. The old stories from the elders and the songs of the glory of the past seemed like nothing more than a dream wished for rather than a time that has passed. It's almost incomprehensible to the point it's unbelievable how the enviable world of grandeur they were told they once lived in transformed to this pitiable state of squalor. How could this happen if the world was as great as their elders' stories described it to be? The younger freed slaves were told all the time that they were created for more. This is what the elders told the younger free slaves daily. The reality is that hard labor is almost all most of the younger people ever saw or could even remember. Mostly, slavery is all they have ever known and all that most will ever know. This was the typical reality of what most free blacks faced every day in their new reality of being free. They had become accustomed to a life of catering to and living in fear of the non-blacks.

Southern life was a truly humiliating existence for African Americans. If you were born in the north, you only heard stories of what was happening in the south from someone who had escaped. And if you lived in the south, you only heard the stories of what life was like for blacks in the north. Mostly, not too many blacks from the north had been to the south themselves, so they could not tell if the stories were true or not. And for the many so-called freed slaves that escaped the south. They never really talked about their life experiences as they lived in constant fear of being returned to the hell that they had fled away from. It's easy to say you're free, but when you finally make it to where freedom truly is, you understand exactly what you have been kept away from for so long. Knowing this makes you so much more scared that someone will take your freedom back on some unknown technicality. So, because of the fear they lived with every day, the escapees never talked about the road to true freedom. Many only trusted their closest family with the secrets of their escape to freedom. Although this was the case, there were always some who would speak out against the horrors of life for blacks in the deep south.

Life was the same every day for Sampson; he never thought of doing more or being more. He lived with the fact that they expected him to do hard labor for the non-blacks for the rest of his lifetime. However, there was something inside Sampson that separated him from his peers. He knew he was different; he knew there was an enormous world outside the farm fences with land that stretched as far as the natural eye could see. But he knew as long as he was on that farm, he only existed and, for the most part, the world doesn't even know he is there. It's hard to dream of a place you have never been or yearn for a feeling you never felt. Sampson however, knew that there was more to life than his existence up to that point. His heart told him so, and he believed it. He thought it was for this reason he always felt separated from the rest of his comrades. While they longed to finish work to sit and talk, Sampson would long to sit and stare off into the sunset and wonder what was beyond the other side of the endless hills he was gazing upon. He may have been from the same place as them, born and raised, but he knew he wasn't like them at all; for when work was over, they rested, but Sampson kept right on going. He just switched from their work to his own and he would spend hours making stuff from the scraps of his surroundings. To him, every day was like not existing at all. He felt like he wasn't even alive; it kind of felt like he was dead already. He felt like nothing more than a tool being used for someone else's purpose. Sampson would only come alive after he invented objects and created new inventions. He loved to let his imagination create one-of-a-kind instruments to help his fellow farmers in their everyday life. Although he could do all these things, they still considered him retarded because of his autistic characteristics by modern-day standards. He did not know what it was or how to explain it, but there was a voice calling out to him to be more on the inside of him. Whenever Sampson explained his dreams to anyone, they would always downplay his dream and tell him to stop imagining things and to get on with his work. They would say you can't do this and you can't do that. All you can do is create tools and clean, so stay in your place, boy. As harsh as their words were, Sampson understood it was just them casting their fears on him and he would have none of it.

CHAPTER TWO

Sampson continued to dream despite their talk. He carried on like this for many years, but one day, standing before him, was a man named Jacob. Every time Jacob introduced himself to anyone, he would introduce himself as Mr. Smith. Mr. Smith dresses differently from the normal townspeople and he talks differently as well. It was apparent Mr. Smith was an educated man, as this was obvious from his demeanor. Usually, people who talked with his type of grammar and carried themselves with the type of pride he exudes only came from a black college that was rumored to be deeper in the south. It was said that Mr. Smith had been sent there as a young child to clean the school grounds and maintain the classrooms. He was sent with only the promise of being taught how to read. They agreed to teach him only as much as his condition and his effort would allow. Smith worked his way to the top levels of the school. He started with cleaning the yard and washing the windows, but before it would be all over, he became a prominent teacher and role model there. He talked little as a child because of the defects he contracted in his childhood. As a child, he was dumb and unteachable because of his condition. Not that he was dumb mentally by any means; it was just that Mr. Smith had gotten very sick as a newborn, and as the result, he had a few developmental defects. He never thought of his problems as setbacks. He saw them as obstacles to conquer on the road to his destiny. One of his major obstacles was being deaf in one ear and hard-of-hearing in the other. This defect alone made his language delayed tremendously. Mr. Smith learned to read lips at a young age with astonishing accuracy. He did this by watching the teachers through the old window panes as he cleaned them to sparkle. He would spend every opportunity he had memorizing what he saw on the boards and practicing the words in the mirror as he remembered them being spoken, making sure his lips moved the same way he had seen his teachers' lips move during their lectures. He always knew that he would have to make his opportunities in life, even though they were scarce for most blacks. With that being the reality, he understood with his defects that he would get double the hatred, and opportunities would be twice as hard for him to come by. He started poor and defeated, but over time, he would learn to harness his mental powers. Being around the other kids in the school made him feel like if he could only learn to focus on his defects and conquer them; he would have nothing that would hold him back from an extraordinary life. In his mind, he knew one day he could do all the same things the normal kids did and more if he focused on this intensely. Before Mr. Smith left home, his mother made him promise that he would go to the school and do whatever it takes to make it. She made him promise he would not let his shortcomings stop him and that he would do his best with everything that he attempted. She made him promise he would become an educated man. Although he doesn't remember everything about his childhood, this is one thing he never forgot. His promise to his mother became his doctrine for success. His mother knew if he stayed on the farm, it was more than likely they could sell him to another farm or possibly murder him because of his handicaps. So, for his safety and the best opportunity available to his mom, she sent him to the school to stay. Upon sending him there, she was told he would clean the grounds as a young apprentice to the custodian. Mr. Smith's mother was also told that he will probably never return. She hugged him, kissed him, and sent him on to the man waiting to take him to the school. She kneeled on the dirt road weak with grief and sobbing as he clawed at her dress, screaming, "No I don't want to go, mommy please don't give me away." They both sobbed profusely as they studied each other's faces for the last time. The site was heartbreaking to watch as he was being pulled away to start his journey of hope, a mother's hope for her son. He stared in between the tears that streamed down his face, blurring his vision of her face running behind the bus screaming she was sorry and confessing her love and hopes for him. As she got farther away, he could no longer hear her voice, but he could see her waving goodbye until she eventually disappeared, seeming to almost be swallowed whole by the dust of the road behind the bus. They did not promise to give Mr. Smith any form of education. They did, however, allow him to maybe one day attend classes there. For his mother, this was better than any chance he had on the farm; so she didn't think twice about if he should go or not. Mr. Smith did all janitorial work assigned to him with pride. He studied the blackboards through the window as if he was an actual student. He was never tired of learning; he made it his goal to learn as much, if not more, than the actual students. Although he did not sit in the class, to him, he was as much a part of the class as any student. To him, it would only be a matter of time before he would sit at the desk he so adamantly polished every day for years on end.

In the beginning, Mr. Smith was picked on terribly at the school by the other students with whom he attended the same school. I think what was so hurtful about the whole teasing thing is that everywhere he went; it was always the same. He may have had some defects the other students didn't, but I'm sure they all had some hidden imperfections as well. Unfortunately, they all seem to forget that they all came from the farms and were free slaves just like him. How can we destroy one another when there are so many non-blacks with only one intent and that's to destroy us and exploit us as they see fit? Mr. Smith knew he would never be this type of person. He would always do his best to help anyone who needed it. When he first arrived, he was full of great hope and a secure vision of his future. But as he told his story in his substandard dialect to most that heard it, they ridiculed him and told him to give up and go clean up. They would tell him, "you are a janitor who can barely talk right. You will never amount to anything. That's why you are the janitor." They would say that he didn't belong there and he would always be dumb and he can't change that. I think these words hurt him to the core, but not in the way you would expect them to. He became angry and decided that he would accomplish everything he promised his mother and then some more no matter how difficult that may be. Although he stopped telling people his dream because of their negative response, He never gave up on his vision for himself.

One must come to an understanding that it is not the ridicule that one must prove wrong, but it is to oneself that we must prove ourselves to be right all along. You should never choose a direction based on the beliefs of others. It is only by your beliefs in yourself that the correct path for you can be chosen. Smith made his mom a promise before he left that farm, and he was going to make good on every word. When they would tease and humiliate him because of his shortcomings, he never responded or fought back; Mr. Smith just continued to teach himself. He considered himself a professional at cleaning windows. He was so good at it; he could siphon every lesson that was being taught through the plate-glass window while cleaning them. Mr. Smith refused to let the windowpane become a barrier to his education. He decided he would become educated no matter what it took. He absorbed whatever lesson that was being taught at the time like a sponge. He practiced his writing skills on the blackboards before he washed them. He would often rewrite every sentence under the one written to improve his handwriting abilities. In the beginning, he did not know what he was writing as he could not read. Although he could not read, he knew his writing would be a valuable tool in his arsenal. Knowing this in his heart, he practiced every chance he got. Eventually, he learned to read and write with excellent penmanship and speak with proper grammar. By the age of fifteen, he had developed a following at the school as he was becoming known for his excellent speaking skills and tremendous knowledge of many subjects. The interesting thing is that he was neither taking any classes nor had he ever taken one. He had a reputation for cleaning the classrooms but was never known to sit in one. So many who saw his progression over the years were astonished because they could not figure out how this was possible. No one ever saw him study or read anything; so it dumbfounded them at his rapid acquisition of knowledge. He would do his job perfectly. His boards were the cleanest, and he always swept the floors to perfection and the desk was always supremely polished. <u>But just despite how hard he worked on the duties he was assigned, he worked even harder on himself.</u> Mr. Smith became a master at learning in private for fear of being accused of stealing lessons. He loved all the subjects being taught. He learned social studies and became in-depth on the social injustices meted against the blacks in the south. Mr. Smith studied the techniques used by the non-blacks to oppress his people, hoping to keep them from ever truly being free. He understood that<u> the best way to hide the true</u>

potential of a mind's power was to restrain the mind from thinking constructively. He understood the best way to do that was to deny the privilege to read because as long as you never learn the truth, you will only know the world as they create it for you. The world created for him and his people was nothing less than dismal old slavery without the chains. It seemed like nothing more than a cruel joke to the so-called free people.

How can you say I'm a free man or woman but still suffer the same injustice, inequality, and hardships I did as a slave? What exactly did they get freedom from? Tell me; I will wait. If you have no history of where you come from or who you are, then you will believe you are what you are told or taught. You can protest and beg to differ, but if your facts are the same ones being provided to you by your oppressor, there is no argument. If these are the only facts you have, then you have no proof that you are not what they say you are. Slaves needed to never be allowed to dream or develop a sense of hope. The slave owners knew that if slaves thought like free men and women, they would soon demand all the things that a free man requires. The non-blacks knew that if this became contagious and spread like a plague from farm to farm, it would be devastating to these plantation owners who exploited the so-called freed people. The thing about knowledge is that knowledge gives sight to the oppressed mind. Knowledge allows the receiver to lift their head from its clouded perceptions of life and begin to form a vision for themselves. While obtaining this new vision for one's life, they realize they must deconstruct the mirage of oppression that was forced upon their reality. It is through knowledge that you learn your surroundings are only what you allowed them to be, and we all have the opportunity to change things if we really choose to. The one thing the taskmasters understood clearly is that knowledge is freedom, and it must be protected at all costs. So, for this reason alone, they burned black schoolhouses down in the middle of the night. The smart blacks who taught anything were killed by lynching and left to hang in the open. This was done to strike fear into the freed people's hearts and make them resistant to even the thought of being taught. So to the freed people, the outcome for trying to learn didn't seem like it was worth it all. This thought process became entrenched in the mind of the blacks over time. It was so ingrained into their thought process that they began to torment their own for wanting to learn. They would abuse their people for wanting to be smart and craving an education claiming they wanted to be like Massa. This was the biggest atrocity that was forced on people of color back then. It was so hammered into the logic of the freed people that until this day, the stigma still carries on in our modern neighborhoods. Neighborhoods that talk properly and get an education are considered acting white. Please think for a minute how sad that whole outlook is that being black meant you had to be dumb. They had us fooled that to seek an education was trying to become someone else. The worst part about the whole thing is that non-blacks did not always need to be present to keep the mentality alive. All they had to do was institutionalize their subordinates' thinking and they would willingly oppress one another as well as themselves. If you wanted to read or write, you were picked on, called names, and some of the blacks even reported you and you would be killed. It was very important for a slave not to talk too much about their ambitions for learning. It was a very dangerous decision and one not to be taken lightly under any circumstances. It was well known that saying yes to the calling to learn could cost you your life if you were found out. Smith also prevailed in math and science and became an avid astronomer as well. He could plot the constellations just by looking at the stars. Mr. Smith was becoming a very intelligent young man but suppressed a lot of his knowledge for fear of being accused of stealing lessons.

CHAPTER THREE

There was a teacher who taught African American studies at the school, Mr. Williams. Mr. Williams was a tall man with a thick curly Graybeard and curly hair who wore the same two suits every day. The suits were a black one and a gray one that had been worn so much that they were coming apart at the seams but he wore them anyway. His teaching shoes were black and shined to a mirror finish. His other pair that he so happily called his walking shoes did not resemble the same care as the black shoes. Mr. Williams had only two pairs of shoes in his possession and never wanted any more. The black shoes he never wore outside due to the dust and dirt; he only wore them in class. He promptly removed his shoes after every lecture day and polished them, then he would wrap them in an old sackcloth and put them back in his drawer for the next day of class. He would put on his walking shoes that he walked so long in that there were holes in the bottoms. If you ever walk close enough behind Mr. Williams you could see his feet through the holes in the soles of his shoes. This didn't stop him from putting the shoes on. It didn't matter what condition they were in or what the weather was; he wore the shoes anyway and he always wore them with pride. Though his shoes were worn out, he refused to replace them. He would place pieces of cardboard at the bottom of his shoes to keep his feet from going through the bottom. He would walk home in those shoes every single day with a smile on his face greeting everyone he passed with a vibrant hello. He was an amazing teacher that was very well respected by the town that was built around the college. The town shoemaker maintained Mr. Williams' black shoes he kept in his desk at school and made sure that they were always in Tip-Top shape. Mr. William didn't have to pay the shoemaker but he always did. He kept his old shoes on his feet and never had them looked at. It didn't matter how the shoemaker would offer to clean those shoes and fix them; he would not take them off for anything.

He would always say these shoes are fine and made to walk in their purpose. Before I am done and I need a new pair, I will have reached the end of this journey, finally arriving at my expected destination. The shoe smith never knew what Mr. Williams meant but he respected Mr. Williams so much that he dare not ask for him to explain. Mr. Williams was considered one of the smartest men in that community; so any time he came to visit the Shoemaker, the Shoemaker would <u>always listen more than he ever spoke.</u> He never wanted to be considered illiterate by Mr. Williams. Although it was an honor for the Shoemaker to work on any pair of shoes that Mr. Williams had, he dared not to pressure him to remove his walking shoes out of respect for the greatness of such an incredible man. But the shoemaker would always remind Mr. Williams that if he ever got ready for the shoes to be looked at to bring them to him, he would fix them up for free. Mr. Williams would always respond the same way, he would say "When this walk is finished, I'll bring them in for you to refurbish them".

The shoemaker always asked, "Well, when do you think that will be? I just want to make those a bit more comfortable for you." Mr. Williams said "I will know it when I have arrived, and surely when I get there, you will hear of my completion as well," he said with a soft smile. Then he took his shiny black shoes and wrapped them up in a sackcloth and went about his way home. He lived in a little one-bedroom shack that he built himself when he first moved into the town. It was built behind the school on a piece of land that was given to him by the school for his dedication to educating all that entered there. Mr. Williams could be seen every day walking through town to the storehouse and back. Many people would give him shoes and clothes that he always accepted with a smile but he never wore. He always gave the donations he received to the class of fresh faces that came to the school throughout the years. He would always give the new students this quote when he gave out the clothes. "To occupy a new space, one must first retire his old positions," he would say "To move into your future, you must first move past the boundaries of your past". He would always tell them that one may never find who he truly may become if he only sees himself through the clouded vision of his past and where he has been instead of where he can go. For the many students that came into contact with Mr. Williams over the years, all of them developed endearing respect for him. They admired his knowledge and quotes that he seemed to never run out of. In the beginning, honestly, the students didn't quite understand what Mr. Williams meant by all of his fancy talks. The new students would always think Mr. Williams was just giving out philosophy quotes as a bonus with the clothes and shoes he was handing out. It would take a while but eventually, the students would realize that the quotes were not just mere sayings but intricate directions on how to develop a new perspective for living life. He always gave any clothes and shoes that were gifted to him to all that needed them. The townspeople never knew quite why he did it but they loved that he would do it.

CHAPTER FOUR

One day as Mr. Smith or Tommy as he was known as a child back then was cleaning the Blackboards in a classroom, Mr. Williams walked in. When Mr. Williams walked in and saw Tommy reading and studying the lecture that he had just taught a few hours before. He said in a loud stern voice, "What exactly are you doing son?" Tommy looked at him with eyes as wide as silver dollars and a face of shock as he trembled before Mr. Williams'. Tommy could not speak or even Gather his thoughts on what he would say. It seemed as if the words had been sucked right out of his head. He was frantically moving his mouth but no words were coming out. He stood in shock for what seemed like an eternity. He looked in disbelief at scenes from his childhood as they played in his head. He also remembered his mother's words like it was yesterday when she spoke them to him. He could almost hear her voice as the words he promised her were being broadcast over his mind like a loudspeaker.

As tears began to roll down his face, the fear of being fired and kicked out of the only place he found accepting of his defects was starting to kick in. He stood frozen as if time had stopped. The moments seemed to linger forever in the uncomfortable silence. In Tommy's mind, this one lapse in judgment was about to cause him everything that he had hoped for. His quest for knowledge was going to be the reason he destroyed everything that he was working towards. This one mistake was going to put everything he dreamed of in jeopardy. He watched his hope for a better future and life float away like the dust particles suspended in the dry hot air of the classroom. The warm tears were running down his face and instantly cooled by the breeze from the open window nearby. He had been there since the age of seven and he knew he would be a disappointment to his mother if he had been kicked out and had to return to the farm. He had been receiving a small stipend for the work he did on campus which he happily sent back to his mom and the rest of his family to help care for them. He only fondly remembers the family he only got to hear from through two letters he received a year. As the scene played in his head, the feeling of shame began to weigh heavy on his heart. While still revisiting his past in his mind, Mr. William Stern's voice came rushing through his fog of memories like a raging river. In his deep-toned voice, he said, " Son, come on out with it, a fool is only perceived as a fool if others don't know who he is and I know you're no fool; now answer the question." Tommy looked at him and with tears covering his face and his mouth bone dry being moistened by the saltwater that came from his eyes, he said in a low voice, "I just wanted to learn sir." "Well, is this how you do it, sneaking around and reading the lectures of teachers in classes you didn't attend," roars Mr. William's stern voice. Tommy became weak with fear and almost collapsed to the floor from the burden of guilt. "No sir," he stated as his eyes were so filled with tears that his vision was now completely blurry. Mr. Williams responded again, "Stand up straight son, there is no representation of pride in the cowering." Tommy stood up straight. Mr. Williams asked him "Who told you I own these words?" Tommy Was confused, he didn't understand the question. Mr. Williams asked again even more directly, "Who told you that I own these words?" Tommy just stood there. Then Mr. Williams asked Tommy another question. "You read my writing on the blackboard but who do the letters belong to?" Tommy, breathing shallowly and rapidly, said in an almost whisper, "They belong to you, sir. Mr. Williams yelled out, "A man that is afraid to speak does not deserve to be heard." Or maybe he just doesn't have anything of importance to say and if that's the case, by all means, be quiet." Tommy responded, "They belong to you, sir." Now more eloquent and slightly audacious. Mr. Williams fired right back almost instantly. "Who told you that I own these letters or words?" Tommy looked startled as he responded, "Sir, you wrote them on the board during your lecture." Mr. Williams responded, "Words belong to no man they are a gift to all who seek to obtain them." Mr. Williams further asked Tommy, "What are you crying about? Are you ashamed of something? Are you ashamed that I caught you reading my work?" In a low voice, Tommy said, "yes sir". Mr. William said with the same stern tone, "I told you before: a man who Whispers his truth does not have anything of importance that needs to be heard." Tommy spoke up, "yes yes yes sir," with a slight stutter. He looked at Mr. Williams with the fear of 100 men plastered across his face waiting on the outcome of this conversation. Mr. Williams said with a stern voice, "a man should never be ashamed to learn, but he should always be ashamed to stay who he is. Do you believe that?" Tommy responded, "Yes sir." Mr. William said, "You have cleaned this school for years. Don't you deserve the education of your peers?" "Yes, sir," Tommy said, looking at the ground. <u>"Hold your head up Tommy, you have nothing to be ashamed of. The only thing that you should be ashamed of is that it took you so long to realize that you deserve to learn like the rest of us. We are all average people striving to be incredible human beings. We are striving to not be trapped by our past, but instead encouraged by the possibilities of our futures</u>." And with that being said, Mr. Williams turned around and walked away. However, before fully leaving Tommy's presence, Mr. Williams stopped and without turning around to face Tommy, said, "Your lesson will be on the board every day, <u>learn it until it becomes you</u>." Then Mr. Williams continued in the direction of the exit and from that day forward Mr. Williams and Tommie Smith became very close friends. Mr. Williams would always leave work on the board and he spent many days teaching Tommy Smith to properly read and eloquently speak. Tommy was a fast learner and over time, became Mr. Williams' assistant teacher. When Tommy became fluent in reading, he was introduced to the library where he became fluent in African American literature. He was fascinated by how the human body worked and became astute in human anatomy and physics as well. He loved to study many different aspects of The Human Condition.

Tommy would eventually become the head of the science department and he lived together with Mr. Williams in the house Mr. Williams had built. Mr. Williams showed Tommy how to build an additional room onto his house and they lived there for the next 15 years. One day while getting ready to teach, Mr. Smith as he was now being called,heaped thanks to Mr. Williams For his guidance. Mr Smith called out to Mr. Williams. As he did every morning, he was reminded of the time Mr. Williams had told Tommy, "You should never introduce yourself as Tommy again." He explained to Tommy, "You are Mr. Smith. Tommy is no longer the height of your reach. That moment in time that this name represents shall never bar you from reaching your higher self again. Mr. Smith is everything you are meant to become and the options are endless for him. While getting ready for the lecture Mr. Smith called out to Mr. Williams again as he did not answer the first time. "It's time to get up old man, we got lives to change" Mr. Williams never responded. Mr. Smith walked over and touched Mr. Williams. His body was cold as ice and lifeless. Apparently, Mr. Williams had died peacefully in his sleep. Mr. Smith began crying heavily over Mr. Williams' lifeless body begging him not to go. He wailed in agony thinking about how he was not ready to walk his path alone. Mr. Smith looked at the old shoes Mr. Williams would wear everywhere he went and he finally realized what that quote Mr. Williams would always say meant. You see Mr. Williams had got those shoes off his father when he was killed in front of his house when he was still a boy. Mr. Williams wore those shoes every day in remembrance of the walk towards education his father started but never got to finish.

The two suits were the only suits his father had other than his field clothes. He had saved his money for three years to get the two suits because he had dreams of being a teacher in the town where they lived. So you see the shoes and Suits meant more to him than many knew. He wore them to honor his father's Legacy and to remind himself of exactly what he could accomplish if he put his mind to it. Mr. Smith buried Mr. Williams in his black suit and folded his gray suit and put it under his head as a pillow in case he needed another suit on his new Journey. Also accompanying Mr. Williams on his new Journey were his walking shoes with the holes in the bottom. But before Mr. Smith placed them on Mr. Williams' feet for the last time, he had them cleaned and polished to a shine. He had the souls of the shoes removed and replaced because he wanted Mr. Williams to start his walk on his new Journey with new shoe soles to match. He could almost envision Mr. Williams reaching his new destination in comfort and style. Many people from many various countries from all over the world came back to say goodbye to Mr. Williams. I think it was finally becoming apparent to Mr. Smith that this old man he spent so many days learning from had changed many more lives than just his own. He had a whole world of people who thought the world of him. And now that Mr. Williams is gone, they shall live on in the new world that Mr. Williams had created. It was a world where every man has a chance if he believes in himself. Mr. Williams' philosophy was that every person has a chance to succeed if only he believes enough in himself and strives to achieve it. Before meeting Mr. Williams, many of their worlds were small and only consisted of poverty and hard labor as this was their only outcome to their situation. But through him, their lives were forever changed and their outlook on life was made much brighter than they ever could have imagined. Mr. Smith gave the closing remarks at Mr. Williams Funeral and he said "I was lost and desolate, deprived of Hope and feeling trifled by life. Mr. Williams gave me hope when <u>he watered my dreams and sprouted a destiny from the dirt of a former life.</u> I thought I had no dreams and for me, there was no good end. But <u>with his words, he took an unkempt mind and groomed this forever changed free-thinking man</u>. He once told me I should only be ashamed to stay the same, so I vow I shall never be the same again. <u>With books, I grow my mind so I embrace them at every chance I get. I used to be a scared boy ashamed of my shortcomings, but now I understand, that it was these shortcomings that he used to form the greater man.</u>" He wept softly as he read this poem ending it with, "I'm not crying because I am afraid of what life has to offer, I cry because I can never truly repay and thank a mighty great friend." He continued to teach his class at the University for the next 3 years.

CHAPTER FIVE

Then one day without notice, he put up his resignation and decided to go into the world and change the lives of all who were willing to be taught. He vowed to teach all that were willing to learn but could not afford the education. He took the black shoes that had formerly belonged to Mr. Williams and he carried them under his arm as he walked down the dusty road. His shoes in one hand wrapped in the same cloth that Mr. Williams used to carry his shoes in and a briefcase in the other hand. With his tools of the trade, he set off to make his mark on the world. Before entering a town Mr. Smith always wore the pair of shiny black shoes as he wanted to look every part of the educated man he was.

One day, as he entered a new town, he was walking down the street with his briefcase in one hand and his walking shoes in his other hand and he saw something strangely familiar. Walking through town, Mr. Smith caught Sampson's attention because he was dressed in a way different from any man Sampson had ever seen before. He and Mr. Smith locked eyes with each other and for that split second, Mr. Smith saw what he could have been and Sampson Jacob saw what he could be if he could educate himself. Mr. Smith was taken aback by the contraption that Sampson was using. It was a little handheld crank primitive in design but effective in its purpose. It had a wheel on it and it had little claws that were made out of wire hangers. Sampson seemed to bring his oddly constructed invention to life as he was using it to pick the cotton in the field he was working in. He was twice as efficient as the others who worked by hand. This was the first time Mr. Smith had seen anything of its kind. It instantly reminded him of going from farm to farm to clean barns. He had only small memories of people picking cotton by hand as he had mostly stayed in town and never visited the outer countryside or little towns that were spread all around him. He was too young to remember what everyday life was like as he left there so young. Mr. Smith was so used to living in the little town that it might as well have been a walled-in city. Because he has never left since he arrived, when he was watching Sampson collect cotton in such an interesting manner, he was surprised and shocked at what he saw. He was amazed by the technology at work but what he didn't know was that Sampson was an inventor.

Sampson had all kinds of things that made work life easier for him and the people around him. He could take useless items of garbage and other objects he found lying around and build devices that no one had ever seen and they all worked. He was smart in ways that the regular people had never seen. To them, Sampson made incredible contraptions but to Sampson, he was just messing around. I guess it's hard to see your gift when it's in you and you don't know who you are. Sampson knew he was gifted but he had no idea how to make his gifts work for him so he could live his destiny. When Sampson saw Mr. Smith, he saw an escape from life as he knew it to be. He came to the realization real quick that if he left this farm and followed Mr. Smith, then maybe he would have a chance at living a whole new life. He dropped everything he was doing immediately and ran as fast as he could after Mr. Smith until he caught up to him. Once he caught up to Mr. Smith, he said, "show me how to be great." Mr. Smith looked at him and asked him, "What makes you think I'm great?" Sampson replied in a hurry as if he was being timed, "Your clothes sir, I never saw a suit like that and your shoes are so clean. Surely, you did not come from around here. I have never seen another black dress

like you. Surely, you must be someone great."
Mr. Smith said, "Many men have been led
astray, then sold into slavery and many others
killed following the appearance of a man.
Never judge a person by their clothes
because even a fool can look nice if you dress
him that way." He further added, "One should
always judge a man by his character and his
interactions with others as they will give a
clear view to the person behind the outer
appearance."Most of all listen to the words a
man speaks because they always give you a
picture of his true intentions. The words of a
man's mouth will always preview what's really
in his heart over time, Mr. Smith continued.
Sampson responded, "I never met another
black man who spoke like you or dressed like
you before. Teach me to be smart like you."
Mr. Smith said, "Now you're onto something; if
I showed you how to look smart, you could
only portray that image for a moment or until
you opened your mouth and get exposed for
being a fraud. If I teach you to be smart you
can be that way for a lifetime and no man
could ever separate this knowledge from you
no matter how strong he was." And with a
smile and a look of compassion in his eyes,
Mr. Smith turned away and began to walk
down the street. Sampson, being confused,

wasn't sure if he was supposed to go back home to the field or follow him. A few moments went by and Sampson made up his mind that he was going to follow Mr. Smith no matter where he went. He began screaming after Mr. Smith, "Please wait for me, Mr. Smith, I'm coming with you." Mr. Smith continued walking like he had not heard anything at all. He didn't even miss a beat. By the time Sampson caught up with Mr. Smith down the road, he was out of breath and could barely speak. Mr. Smith turned around hastily with a frighteningly serious look on his face and sternly asked him "Why are you following me? I don't owe you anything". Sampson looked at him and said, "I don't want to stay here forever. Show me the way to this freedom that you have found. I want you to teach me to be a man just like you." Mr. Smith responded, "<u>A man must be smart enough to understand when life-changing opportunities are at hand and grasp the moment because it may never come again</u>. I have met many before you that said they wanted the same thing. But they never understood <u>freedom is firstborn in your mind. We can want and long for many things but it is what we hold steadfast in our minds that we shall receive</u>. So many cry freedom, but think poverty and slavery conditions. Because of their thoughts, the things that they don't want, they shall have more of regardless of their bold and spirited confessions. Some things only come to us once, so it is imperative that we understand when that thing is within our grasp." With those words, Mr. Smith turned around and started walking again. Sampson followed directly behind Mr. Smith as he walked. Sampson eventually caught up and matched Mr. Smith's pace and from that point on he walked side by side with him.

His first informal lesson began right at that moment and it was, "If one is truly willing to be taught, he will leave his comforts and move at a pace that is necessary for him to gain the knowledge he knows that he deserves. Never expect greatness to come and find you in your debauchery for many fools have died waiting for their time to come, only to realize in death that greatness sat waiting and praying for them to show up. Do your dreams have more faith in you than you? You were so busy waiting, you never did anything towards your dream. But the crazy part is that your dream was so confident in you that it followed and enticed your mind repeatedly because it knew with you, it could become reality. But the sad truth is that you never became so neither did your dreams. That is such a shame and loss to the whole of humanity. Intellect will never come to where you are, one must always be willing to go after it with a raging thirst that can never be quenched." Smith began to teach Sampson everything he knew starting that day and also for the next 10 years. Sampson followed Mr. Smith as they went from town to town and Sampson absorbed all Mr. Smith's lectures and teachings. Mr. Smith taught Sampson how to read and once he learned how to read, he was considered to be learned by former slave standards. He began to study the mechanics of how the body works and how things operate within the body. He also studied cell structure and all aspects of the human body. Sampson saw a lot of people die in the fields from sickness and infections from wounds they had obtained while working on farms with the equipment. He watched many blacks dying from the same things the whites were being cured of. He wanted to learn how to help the people he felt no one cared about. He would always sit in on lectures he came across in the different towns he visited. He would visit hospitals and there, he learned of many new diseases and the procedures that were being used at the time. Over time,

Sampson became well known in the many places he visited. He was known for his expertise in medicine but only on the rule farms he visited as that was the only place he could practice.

Rumors were going from town to town where he had never been but they held rumors of a black doctor that helped many. Most who heard this story considered it a myth or to be made-up because blacks were not allowed to read and everybody knew this. So a black doctor sounds like an impossible dream that would never be obtained. The whites believed it was just another fake story black people used to give one another hope because most of them had not seen him as well. Mr. Smith was also known throughout the towns he visited as well. But he was known for healing people's minds. He loved to teach his people how to live better and be proud of who they are. He taught them how to carry themselves with dignity and to expect the best from themselves. He always told them to go after whatever they were told they could not do because nothing was impossible. He said, "even though some may say that you can't do it, you should do it anyway." He felt that a man who was not truly living to his fullest potential never really lived. He would say he is already dead and just waiting on his turn for burial. He would also say, "Chase after your dreams for only then are you truly alive and only then can you say you truly lived." He would say, "to learn is to be free; so, one should always strive to learn as much as possible because this is how he guards his mind against the marauders plotting to take everything that is him. Embody the characteristics of the learned and maybe nobody will ever mistake you for a fool again. The reality is, oppression is freely given and always being taught to the masses even without them ever asking." He said it is important to know what freedom feels like, and what it tasted like as well as what freedom smells like. "Learn these attributes and never let them escape your memory. For the day you forget will be the day someone sells you into slavery and you go willingly."

They were known as total body healers in the places where they went. Mr. Jacobs would heal their bodies of ailments as much as he could and Mr. Smith's would focus on healing their minds. Although Mr. Jacobs loved medicine, he still loved inventing as well. So he always had a new invention that he could teach the farm people to use to make their lives a little easier from day to day.

But not everywhere these two men went they were welcome. Some people tried to kill them thinking they were sent to get them into trouble or to be lynched. There were plenty of times that they were chased out of town. It was said that they were almost lynched twice. But I think the worst part about that was that it wasn't being carried out by the whites. Nope, it was being done by the blacks they sought to help. It was done because the other blacks felt that their teachings were dangerous and would get their people hurt. These people decided to remain enslaved if it meant they could live without the fear of hanging. This was not the case but I guess it sounded good to them. The truth is that the freed slaves could be killed for so many things. But I guess it made sense to them not to add another reason for being hated to the list. As if their skin wasn't enough to entice non-blacks to kill, rape, and torture them just for being in the wrong place at that time, it was thought that knowledge only bought death because the ones who did learn were either killed or would mysteriously disappear never to be heard from again. So many blacks wanted no part of learning and tried to kill them in some of the towns they visited but they escaped every time. Mr. Smith and Mr. Jacobs suffered the same treatment from most of the whites they came across during their travels as well. So in a sense, they were never safe anywhere for long but yet, they carried on because purpose outweighs punishment and not even death could kill their dreams.

However, just as there are bad people, there were good people of every race and color in every town these men visited as well. They would always find rest with like-minded people on their travels as well. These two men were attacked and beaten on many occasions on the road while walking from town to town. They would tend to their wounds crawl out of whatever creek or ditch they had been thrown in and the next morning, they would clean themselves off in the river and continue to walk to the next town, never missing a beat, teaching and healing as they went along. Some thought if they beat them badly enough before they got to the town, they would bypass the town, but to their disbelief, they continued undeterred.

One day while walking, Mr. Smith asks Mr. Jacobs a question: "Sampson, are you afraid to die out here?" Sampson replied, "I thought I would never know what living was. I existed so long on these farms doing what my father and his father did. They would say we are free but it never felt that way. I thought we were trapped cursed to never be more, but when I saw you, it was the first time that I was able to see that I can truly be free. I am free for the first time and I truly feel free. I refuse to go back to the farm and exist. This time that I have left, I will live it free as the birds that flew overhead in the fields I used to tend. I will not let the mobs of opposition or their fear of knowledge keep me from becoming all that I can be. I will live free and if I die, I'll die trying. At least, I died for something that meant something to me and not for something that I was told was all I can be. I saw so many great people die working the fields, tending the dreams of our Massa. So when you ask me if I am afraid to die, I will tell you this; 'I was already dead and now I live and when the good Lord sees fit to take me, He can take me living free in all my glory because I am never going back to simply existing again.'" With that being said, they continued with their walk. Mr. Smith couldn't help but think as he walked and talked, teaching along the way how much this young man Samson reminded him of himself.

At that moment Mr. Smith realized that even though Mr. Williams was gone, his spirit was still alive; he could feel his presence in the conversations he had with Sampson. He would always tell Sampson that even though he was a young man, he had a very old soul, meaning his intelligence was beyond his years. They walked and had many talks.

CHAPTER SIX

Sampson Jacobs as he was known, was an avid reader and he continued to read any book he got his hands on. He loved to learn new things and teach them to anybody who would listen. He was fixated on igniting the hunger that he felt every person ever born on this Earth has buried inside of them. His favorite saying was, **"Every person has a dream, some are just buried deeper than others and need more knowledge to sprout**. He loved to call knowledge the Water of Life. He believed that with enough watering, even the deepest dream can Sprout and develop into the life it was meant to become. He always stated that his learning would be done when he has read every book on every subject. He believed that until he accomplished this, he could not ever say his learning was done. But being that there are so many books in the world, he has concluded that he will be learning until the end of time. He learned about most diseases and their molecular makeup of genes and chromosomes although he never went to college. He had a knowledge that rivaled the smartest of white college graduates. He prided himself on his mental capabilities and vowed that he would <u>never go back to being or thinking the way he used to think again.</u> Because to him, **that old way of thinking was the reason for most of his life being spent on the farm picking cotton.** He always felt that he didn't belong there but he was always reminded that that's where he landed and this was his lot in life. So he constantly invented new contraptions to make his life and the fellow farmhand's life better, but he always felt like a fish out of water. In his heart, he felt like he was meant to be more but could not Ponder a way to escape the situation he was in.

Sampson Jacobs loved helping all people; he never turned away anybody. He loved to be the one responsible for giving people a new way to live and a new reason to hope. One day on his walk with Mr. Smith, it finally hit him; he stopped immediately in his tracks. "I see now I am finally understanding many new aspects of my life. But most importantly of all, I am starting to understand my reason for being. <u>All my life, I have been trying to make myself comfortable in my rough situations. I never thought about chasing them away. I was only focused on making myself comfortable and becoming akin to my Agony</u>." He looked at Mr. Smith, his eyes filling with tears. He said, "if it wasn't for you, I would still be trying to make myself comfortable in my pain. But you showed me the way out; it was you who has guided me to the light of my freedom. I can't be who I was ever again. My old, try to make yourself comfortable; your mess thinking died on the farm when I left there. I am a new creature; that old me is gone and may He rest in peace. But the new me, The new man I have become and I am beginning to understand more about day-by-day is wanting to move ahead. I never want to be comfortable again. I shall go from fight to fight but I will never be willing to settle for mess again. <u>I finally understand that nothing changes in your life unless you change it and</u>

<u>that is the only way it changes.</u> I am so ashamed it took me so long to <u>grasp hold of this concept of me as a victor and not the victim.</u> I will always be uncomfortable. I will never be simmered down and accepting of what others think I should have. I will be fighting to become more with every moment and every breath I have left. They cannot defeat me mentally, they can chase me but they can never take my fight away from me. I can learn many new things and become renewed in my thinking every day but I can never forget the old man I used to be. If it was not for his pain of existing, I wouldn't have this insatiable hunger for living. I mourn his hurt. I feel his torment of knowing he didn't belong but I'm so glad for what he had to endure. I will always remember that you can be brutally beaten for something you don't want to do; so why not make the beating worth it. Why would I ever stop moving and teaching out of fear of what could happen or what did happen because nothing can ever be worse than where I came from. At least at this moment, I can say I tasted freedom and it is the sweetest thing I have ever had the opportunity to taste. I think once you have truly tasted freedom, going back to incarceration is just not an option. I forgive my fellow colored Brothers for

the harm and pain they inflicted on me, but I will continue to teach them and reach back for them. They are afraid as I once was. They have been brutalized so much that they are afraid of any kind of change. They are like I used to be trying to remain comfortable in their misery. Maybe the reality we reveal is sometimes too much to take; <u>it's a hard thing to learn that we are the true captors of ourselves.</u> Light hurts the most when you have been chained in darkness for so long that you forget you could see. <u>The only reason we have not progressed past where we have been chained to in society is that we have removed the chains from our legs and padlocked our minds binding us from who we could become.</u> We have stopped being beaten by our masters but now we beat each other to keep us in check and from escaping the hell we have become accustomed to. We are the new Massa. Instead of mastering our minds, we choose to rule and confine one another. I refuse to get into ruling others. I must first learn to control myself. I only want to help my brothers and sisters not be their confinement or the reason they let themselves be confined. Was it not just yesterday that I too was as confused as they are now. I feel like it's my purpose, my reason for living and I will help others learn how to live just as you have shown me." They continue to walk from town to town teaching and healing as the years go by.

Ten years passed and suddenly, there was a new disease that was traveling from town to town like a top-notch salesman but only leaving death behind. It was nothing like anything that had been seen before. It was clear that this epidemic would require their adamant attention. As the disease continued to spread rampantly from farm to farm and eventually from town to town, they were perplexed as to its transmission. They began hearing so many stories of people being taken to the doctor and never coming back. These stories continue to grow as the disease becomes more and more rampant. When the free black people got sick, they tried to keep it a secret, often hiding the sick in their homes until they were too sick or they died. No one trusted the white doctors; they understood that they would never receive good care from them. Some good doctors would try to help all sick but they did not know how to stop the disease or its origin. At this moment, if you had taken a census of doctors, the majority did not care what started it or how to slow its progression. Most had one-track minds that were focused purely on a cure. So their focus was just to manage the symptoms that the disease caused. They would go from farm to farm experimenting on the blacks to find a cure for treating the whites with the elixirs that showed promise. At that time, that is all that they could do with the limited knowledge of the disease they had. They would build sick houses that would have tall fences around them. The sick were kept in beds in the basement. It didn't take long before the houses were full of sickbeds and as the sick died, their bodies would be burned right outside in a large pit for all the sick to see their coming demise. It seemed that anybody who was in contact with them for extended periods would contract the sickness as well. The doctors would not spend much time with the sick as they did not want to contact the disease. They would go to many towns but they didn't visit the farms too often because they were mostly blacks and their offspring. They would only see blacks of prominent background as they had the money to pay for their service. They would send word through Messenger to the slave sick houses where many would lie sick and die. They wouldn't die because someone was not putting forth the effort, no, not at all. They died because most of the time, the medical orders would not be followed correctly. Not because the slave workers did not want to follow the directions, but because the workers could not read. The slaves could not accurately make elixirs or formulate the correct dosage due to this handicap. The measuring equipment might as well have been in Roman numerals because they could not count. A lot of the medications that came from the slave-run homes caused death and the ones that did work quickly went non-existent. They would guess the quantities and assume the ingredients and so with no documentation, it made it almost impossible to duplicate batches.

To say the least, many people died from the affliction. The slaves also killed their fellow people by giving them medication that was taken in the wrong dosage or by the wrong route. It also didn't help that all patients took medications from the same equipment often with no hand washing in between. It was apparent that human suffering was taking a toll on the minds and bodies of the two men. They strive to do more but the reality is that there was only so much that could be done between the two. One day while lecturing, Mr.

Jacobs was approached by a white doctor that was sitting in on one of his lectures as this was not an uncommon sight. The educated blacks were allowed to attend and lecture at these medical conventions; they just had to stand in the back as only the non-blacks were allowed to use the convention seating. So all were welcome and each opinion was respected because it was believed amongst all who enter there that knowledge has no specific race. Because of this common belief, they believed that **skin tone was introduced as a way to keep the ignorant confused and destroy one another with no need of help from the oppressors. They believed that focusing on a skin tone was the best way to slow people of all races from working together towards a commonly beneficial goal.** It's hard to get past your captors' theology that was being passed from generation to generation of hatred of the color of one's skin. One truly awakened to the knowledge of the universe begins to see that not one blade of grass created was wasted. If the universe saw a purpose for the blade of grass, then how much more important is the human who triumphs over nature and tramples such grass under feet. If we take a moment to ponder a thought of such magnitude, it gives us an understanding that we all must have a purpose. **Your existence is significant. I have never seen anything that was created by Nature in nature that did not belong; meaning the creator does not make mistakes. I understand this to be the most precious of laws; it is the law of purpose. This law states that you are here for a reason; you were created for this moment in time. You are a productive answer to a stagnant universal problem faced by many. You're a nurturer to a subdued consciousness. Your job is arousing your mind from its slumber and pushing its limits to accomplish things you never comprehended as a possibility. So I ask you in the middle of this book what your purpose is.** This is the understanding that most educated men of that time arose to in their level of thinking. It does not matter the color of the doctor if the patient lives. It is not of any importance the color of the gardener if one's belly is full of fresh edibles from the garden. Would the complexion of the skin or religious affiliation change the feeling of being satiated from a meal grown by hand and watered from the sweat of one's brow? Small minds have fought over the same small things for centuries. It's like being in the relay race at a never-ending hate marathon. We continuously pass our torch of ignorance from generation to generation. We do this hoping for a better outcome but <u>history can only repeat itself if the wrongs being taught were never learned from then discarded for a better way of thinking</u>. How sad is the human being to have so much potential and yet still be perplexed at the same irrational thinking of their four fathers. We have seen the world advance in so many areas but in this one flawed way of seeing each other, we remain in the stone age. If you turn your head from left to right, then you would see that on most farms and in most towns of this time, the same pathetic thinking existed. <u>Instead of thinking as individuals, the masses have decided to let the chaos of ignorance be their guiding principle.</u> I am sure that this will go on for many generations to come as we'll always have many among us that are ready to follow but very few that are ready to lead. I wonder how a man can live being led never truly understanding that leading is the ultimate freedom. Every human deserves the right to have their thoughts and feelings and to exist in peace for this is a life lived in abundance. A mind enveloped with hatred, anger, and jealousy or filled to the brim with violence is trapped deep in mental incarcerations that become hard to escape. This flawed thinking will only lead to a confined mind that will eventually bath itself in the hatred, racism, and bigotry that was formerly impressed on it. This for many is a life sentence plaguing the mind from a young age from which they never recover. Some wake up and decide I am not going to live and die like this. But not as many as most find it safer to move with the herd instead of against it.

CHAPTER SEVEN

One day, Mr. Smith changed Sampson's name to Mr. Jacobs and told him just as Mr. Williams had told him that Mr. Jacobs was everything he was becoming. As Mr. Jacobs was giving a speech one day, he watched from the stage as a white doctor approached him with a smile on his face, heaping praise unto him for his lecture he had just given on the importance of individualism. The doctor wanted to talk about a device he had created and needed an out-of-the-box thinker that would give his dream at least a good listen. His name was Dr. Sterlingzinger. He was a German Doctor who was studying the outbreak that was rapidly spreading from town to town. He had been studying this new outbreak from a different perspective and felt that he could stop the spreading of the disease but no one took his methods or him seriously. It could have been because he did not socialize in the same circles as them. Or it could have been that he was thinking about a different way of approaching the outbreak than his peers and this is a well-known recipe for ostracization.

The world is funny that way; if you're not doing what everyone else is doing then you're weird. But I guess, dressing, eating, talking, and watching the same things as everyone else is not odd at all. Maybe being oddly shaped carbon copies of each other is ok. I mean an individual with a voice can be dangerous. The doctor had invented a small portable oven that he felt would kill organisms that were on the instruments. He felt that this was the cause of the infection being carried from town to town. Being a doctor who visited all who needed assistance was noble indeed, but he didn't think they understood that their unsanitary techniques were the cause of the rapid spread of the disease. It was for this very reason that the disease would become resistant to the treatments rather quickly. It almost seemed like a different disease from town to town but it was just a mutated strain from the comingling of cells covering the instruments used. The doctor as smart as he was had a major problem that he could not figure out how to overcome with his invention. The problem was that the instruments would get hot due to it being heated by fire; so it was a struggle to regulate the Heat. It also made it dangerous and almost impossible to access the tools once the box got hot. The instruments inside due to the Heat being unregulated left some tools melted and disfigured and others completely ruined during his initial trials. As the doctor continued to talk about his invention and the calamities facing its operation, it was like God was designing the improvements to the oven right before Jacobs's eyes. What the doctor saw as a machine with one purpose, Mr. Jacobs saw many different operations being performed by the same machine. He told the doctor he was positive he could improve on his invention. Mr. Jacobs told the doctor that not only could he improve the design but he could also make it useful in many more aspects than even the doctor had first thought of. When Mr. Jacobs begins to lay out his vision for the crude oven that the doctor had created, he floored the doctor leaving him stunned at how fast he had come up with a solution to his problem he had pondered many nights over.

The design, in the beginning, was a primitive one. It consisted of a metal box held Under Fire with a long pole attached and a latched door that could only be accessed when it cooled off. Mr. Jacob's free way of thinking came up with a design that was going to transform a once amateur device into a state-of-the-art machine. With his thinking style, this box became a three-level chest with drawers that had handles that never got as hot as the chest. On the bottom layer was a drawer that was to be the heating unit; it could hold 2 pounds of wood and 4 gallons of water. On the top layer of the drawer, the wood was inserted. On the left, water was inserted through a pipe. On the right, the next drawer was for the utensils; they were washed and placed in this station drawer. The drawer had holes in it that allowed the steam to essentially steam the parts. This made sterilizing the parts more effective and less damaging. It did not destroy the tools it was tasked with disinfecting anymore as now, the temperature was more regulated. The second level would be the thermometers and the other objects such as bowls, cups, and other handheld items. On the last level, drawer number 3 was used for the heating level as most poor sick houses didn't have proper heating; so he put another 2-gallon pan on top and a tube to fill it, kind of like a smokestack that allows all of the steam and heat to be used. The doctor was amazed at the level of superb knowledge that Samson possessed. The doctor pondered a response that would allow him to keep his dignity and respond with poise. At that moment, the doctor was realizing his dream was about to become much more than he ever could have imagined. He began to weep and just as the doctor could no longer contain the emotions, he leapt and hugged Mr. Jacobs. Mr. Smith watched from the sidelines as he mingled with another group. Smith glared in astonishment at the scene taking place in the hall. What made this doctor so emotional was that he had attended many meetings but never spoke; he only listened. I guess you can say that trying to follow his dream had dealt him some unsettling blows. Being the joke of his peers for his views that were outside the realm of thinking of the doctors around him made him a quiet and withdrawn man. He used to try and explain his theory on the virus composition that seemed to change so rapidly and the direct effects the doctors played in the spread of the disease. But he was usually laughed at and called a fool for his thinking. They would say doctors making patients sicker is the stupidest thing they ever heard. They labeled him a dumb doctor with even dumber views. So for anyone to see him so emotional was out of his character. So Mr. Smith excused himself from the group he was entertaining and made his way towards Mr. Jacobs and Mr. Sterlingzenger. As he walked towards them, he and Mr. Jacobs locked eyes and Mr. Jacobs smiled as his face exuded a peaceful glow. Smith became more at ease at the jester from Mr. Jacobs as it eased his mind as he did not know what to think at first. He wasn't sure if this was another situation that they would have to try and escape with their lives as they did on many other occasions. But that was not the case this time. As Mr. Smith approached the two men embracing each other, the doctor turned to him, and as Mr. Smith held out his hand with a smile, the doctor grabbed his hand and pulled him in for a hug. He repeatedly thanked Mr. Smith for being a magnificent mentor and for crafting such an eloquent human being. He said that Mr. Jacobs is special and he will change so many lives. He said, but that is only half the story he came with you. So if this is what represents you, I must meet your representative himself as he deserves heaps of praise for his hard work and dedication. Who is your teacher because it's obvious you come from great stock and I surely would hope to meet him someday? as well smiling as he asked Mr. Smith. I would love to send him praise for his molding of such a fine gentleman as yourself. I am sure you were crucial in the development of this great man standing here as I have no doubt he will be a blessing for many people in the future. It was your compassion that molded this man as I'm sure someone great molded you. The doctor began to question Mr. Smith about where he was from and how he could be such an inspiration and no one ever noticed. As Mr. Smith began his response, tears began to pour down his face. He tried to speak in muffled words but the only thing he could get out was Williams. The doctor, being confused but caught up in the emotions as well, asked him who Williams was and where he could find him. Mr. Smith said you can't thank him as I can never thank him for seeing something in me that I never knew was there. As the doctor listened, he began to turn red in the face from the built-up emotions he was trying to contain as he understood what Mr. Smith was trying to say. Instantaneously, Mr. Jacobs ran to Mr. Smith and wrapped his arms around his chest and told him, "You have done the same thing for me and I can never repay a man as great as you as well." At that moment, the three men lost all composure and began to cry hysterically as they stood in a circle embracing one another. I am sure, to onlookers, this was probably really strange but each man had their reasons for their emotions being on display in such a manner. Mr. Smith's one ambition in life was to teach someone else to be free the same way his teacher did for him.

At this moment, he realized he did exactly what he was inspired to do most. Free the minds of as many people as he could come into contact with in his lifetime. He never paid attention to his journey but at this moment, at this stop on the road to Destiny, he realized he was right where he dreamed he would be many years before. I'm sure Mr. Williams visited this place as well. It's the place of true enlightenment. It's the place where in that **moment, one realizes his life has been designed for this one moment in time. Even at his darkest moments in life, there was a reason for it. Every pain, every heartache was for this very moment. When you realize that it took all the pains of your past to create the oasis of your future, this can be a very overwhelming experience.** You begin to understand that not one pain or life experience was wasted and every pain and setback had a purpose and was by divine design. I bet Mr. Smith never thought the pain of his life would be the part that would feed Mr. Jacob's dream to become everything he could ever hope to be and more. I think sometimes our pains connect us more than most realize.

The doctor was in shock as he saw his life work finally about to take shape. You see, most thought he was a fool chasing the wrong part of the situation. The doctors in the makeshift hospital thought it was the patient with the symptoms, not the instruments. They said he was a fool for trying to focus on objects instead of the real issue people. With all the ridicule he faced, he still carried on being laughed at for years at a time. He was quickly garnered as a quack but this doctor never gave up on his dream. His wife left him and took the kids. He was alone, just a broken man and his dream of an idea. An idea that nobody thought would work. An idea that made him seem foolish every time he spoke it but yet, he continued with his focus. He has studied bacteria formation and the general makeup of many pathogens. He was very knowledgeable but due to his way of thinking and attacking the epidemic, he was not respected or accepted in the medical community. He was usually ostracized when he gave lectures and laughed at when he would enter institutions. Questioning by his peers usually always ended in him becoming the butt of someone's jokes. Mr. Sterlingzinger no longer visited the makeshift hospitals but instead, he chose to treat people on farms and in the rule outreaches of the towns he visited. It was here he perfected his techniques. He prefers this way of treating the sick anyway. It allowed him to be more on the front lines against the infections that were present in the communities he visited.

By being ostracized and expelled from the group thinking did more for his studies than he could have ever imagined. This is because it allowed him to see the direct effects of using his chosen techniques. It allowed him to study disease progression as well as the symptoms and the medications that work best for many different ailments. He studied the structure of the cell hoping to find weaknesses or flaws that made the cells readily destroyable. He documented all of his findings and created his book called the Cure-All. He named it this because he believed with his documentation of diseases and their characteristics and his techniques for infection control and utensil sterilization, he could go to any town that was dealing with an outbreak and stop the outbreak from spreading any further. He believes his techniques could lower the death rate in any place that was plagued by sickness. Because it took very long for word to spread of this doctor's triumphs, he remained in obscurity. He only obtained fame in the small towns he visited, but talking to Mr. Jacobs, he saw his life was finally about to change. Not only did he find someone that could help him bring his invention to life and improve on it but the most important thing was that he found someone who believed in him. Someone who saw his vision and would help him achieve it for him; this is the chance to bring his procedures to a bigger audience with results to boost his credibility but also with a machine to aid his triumphant achievement. So his tears represented a chance to finally be validated; it would also clear his name and restore his family's dignity. So to the doctor, this was more than just building a contraption; it was validating a life's purpose. This was going to be the start of a whole new generation of procedures and equipment that was going to change the way care was provided. It would be this chance encounter that would solidify this day as the day that all of his life's work would finally be on display for the world to see and learn from. And the world was going to see just how much of a genius this man they laughed at and tormented daily truly was. The tears the doctor was shedding were not only grief but it was also for the coming vindication that he knew he would justly receive.

Mr. Smith, holding his composure together as much as possible erupted and began sobbing so intensely that he collapsed into the arms of the doctor; his emotions were on full display as well. Mr. Jacobs continued to weep as he held on tight. Mr. Smith tried to talk but could not speak in between the tears and heavy breathing in his unfiltered emotions. The emotion was too much for even tough men like them to contain. He continued to try to talk and the doctor said I know as he looked Mr. Smith in the eyes and they continued to weep uncontrollably. Pain lived does not need words to be understood; there is a familiarity with pain you have gotten to know personally. When you get a chance to visualize this kind of pain, you know it is just as one knows a family member that has moved away; though they have gone, they are not forgotten.

Mr. Jacobs was nothing special in the town he was from. He had not many friends and the friends he did have just ridiculed him. He stayed mostly to himself inventing gadgets out of the scrap he found lying around. Mr. Jacobs was a Hands-On learner who loved to learn from watching others. If he saw you do anything once, he could do it as well as you could on his first try. He could fix almost anything by taking it apart. He loved reading books after he learned how to read. <u>Mr. Jacobs consider reading his duty; he would say, "All these years, I was dumb; I shall never give life that opportunity to handle me foolishly again. I shall create my destiny and no longer be its victim of circumstance."</u> Mr. Jacob loves to read but then, again, one could say he got it from Mr. smith. Mr. Smith loved reading on many subjects. It was this very gift that allowed both Mr. Smith and Mr. Jacobs to grasp the concepts of subjects instantaneously; he could read a book once then teach the key points of that book to perfection. He and the doctor became very close.

Because Mr. Jacob and the doctor were spending multiple hours together working on their sterilizing station. The doctor would use this time to lecture Mr. Jacobs on the characteristics and progression of many diseases. He would teach him their cell structure and the defects that made them attackable. He also explained in detail what treatments were most effective for each situation and why. He taught him the importance of a sterile environment and the proper way to disinfect the tools. Mr. Jacobs over time became very intelligent in the things of medicine. He became known as a healer in a lot of the rule towns; some would call him a witch doctor with healing potions. I think they called him a witch because people are afraid of what they don't understand. I think that a lot of times, instead of trying to understand a thing, people tend to vilify it or disregard it as dangerous due to their lack of understanding. They rather call someone's hard work magic rather than understand and praise them for the years of dedication it takes to perfect one's craft. **This is the Achilles heel of humanity; we always label something mythical or say the receivers of good fortune are lucky. We never take into account the many years they worked or honor them for their dedication to purpose**. Rather than work the years in obscurity, we try to put on your shoes and wear your robe and think we should get the same talents you worked years for. Sadly, this is not the case; this is not how success works but the world keeps on trying to become something this way anyway. And thus, we have found the ultimate path to retarding our progression on the road to evolution as we all prefer the easy garbage instead of the high-quality life we all can work towards.

CHAPTER EIGHT

Mr. Jacobs, Smith, and the doctor would travel together for a total of three years as it took this long to get the machine up and running and they use the rural farmer as testing grounds for their procedures as well as their contraptions. By the end of the three years, word began to spread about this white doctor and his machine that bought health and heat at the same time. At least, this is how the Layman people explained it, but to the doctor, it was so much more than this. Although Mr. Smith and Mr. Jacobs were with the doctor, they were barely ever mentioned as creators of this contraption. They were just considered to be the doctor's help. This never bothered any of the three men because as long as Mr. Jacobs was learning, he could care less about the glorification. It was the knowledge to heal his people that Mr. Jacobs wanted more than anything. He felt that his task in life was much more critical than receiving the praises of other men. Mr. Smith loves the excitement of bettering his people and passing along the hunger for knowledge and the desire to be more than they were yesterday. The doctor cared about stopping the way hospitals and sick houses carried out the care of their sick. He wanted to stop the innocent that suffered and died needlessly from improper care of hazardous materials and poorly cleaned instruments.

All these men had their reasons for becoming who they were. But most of all, they cared deeply about their fellow human beings; this reason alone kept them together. Their love for their fellow people propelled them along on their quest to end suffering on the level that God had assigned for them. As the world begins to catch up on the success of the doctor, his techniques and his machine, the doctor became relatively famous overnight. His machine was now the talk in big cities and his techniques became very well known. He became famous all around the world; his technique was coined after him and called the sterile technique and his cleaning method was called sterilization named after him as well. He never forgot what good camaraderie he had with his two dear friends and he spent the rest of his life teaching and selling his invention. He always made sure to keep in touch with Mr. Jacobs and Mr. Smith as he always sent them money every month. As a doctor, he made sure the men had the money for supplies as they continued from town to town. Mr. Smith carried his briefcase with his good news and his shoes up under his other arm that he only wore now during lectures and Mr. Jacob carrying his doctor's bag of hope and a briefcase full of lectures. The doctor would send Jacob lectures he would write for him. He would tell him about the new medications and treatments as he was always learning and further perfecting his techniques in the bigger cities. For this reason, Mr. Jacob was always up on top of the latest news on bacterial outbreaks and medications used in viral repression. The two men, Smith and Jacobs had become famous in their own right, becoming sort of aristocrats to the affluent African American people of their time. They were very well known in these circles; their reputations far preceded them.

Time continued to pass and one day, Mr. Smith started to become ill. He had been around the sick and lectured enough to know the signs of the disease he had contracted. He knew enough to know about his symptoms and to understand what his expected outcome would be. He hid his sickness from Mr. Jacobs as he knew there was no cure. Mr. Jacobs had just received an invitation from the league of black Scholars to attend a banquet. He was confused as he had never heard of them and could not understand how the group knew of him or heard of his many medical miracles as the freed would call them. Mr.

Smith told him he should be honored to receive such an invitation as this.

The virus that's affecting the rural population no longer spreads with the doctor's sterile techniques. It tremendously slowed the spread but it still had a high mortality rate. The big city doctors were mostly confused about the outbreak; so they didn't visit the outskirts of town much as they did not want to infect themselves or their families. They would have a chalkboard at every sick house on the porch so the doctor never even had to enter into a sick house anymore. They wrote instructions on these boards for the people who cared for the sick to follow until they return. Most of the caregivers were slaves and couldn't read and most of the whites that were there could not read either. The whites were considered the poor whites and were treated only slightly better than the blacks. As the big night for the banquet was finally approaching Mr. Smith had been in bed all day. Mr. Jacobs could sense that there was something wrong but did not want to pry, so he just left it unsaid. Mr. Smith smiled widely upon laying eyes on Mr. Jacobs and told him, "I have a request." Mr. Jacobs, wondering what it was, responded, "surely, whatever you need, I will get for you.

You have kept me and for that, I owe you my life." Mr. Smith smiled wide as his eyes began to water; he told Jacob, "son, I'm so proud of all that you have become. I would have never thought that I could be a part of the creation of something so great, but you truly are a great man and I'm so honored to know you." Mr. Smith got up and slowly walked to the closet where he pulled out the shoes he gave lectures while wearing. He placed them on Jacob's lap. Jacob began to tremble as tears poured down his face; he responded in a broken voice, "I could never take these, they are your prized possession." Mr. Smith responded that these shoes were given to me by a great man. They reminded me every time I put them on why I fight for freedom and teach individualism. These shoes come from my teacher who saw much more than the defective slave child he met me as. A great Man once wore these shoes and now, I give them to you to carry on our walk. The long walk down the path to healing and molding our people. I have given so much and now it's your turn to continue this path that we have chosen. I am not feeling well and I wanted you to have this because I want you to understand just how important you are to me and this cause we are fighting for. He put the shoes on

Jacob's lap and gave him a black suit that was made for him by the town's tailor without him knowing. Mr. Smith told Jacob that the shoes were meant for him to have as he looked Jacob in the face, his voice cracking under the pressure of the emotions he was carrying and attempting to conceal. He told Jacob, "I could never in a million years find a man more worthy of these shoes than you are. You have represented everything a great man is supposed to be and I swear to you this day that if my teacher ever met you, he would be just as proud as I am.

Mr. Jacobs had always admired the shoes ever since he first saw Mr. Smith walk into town some twenty years ago. He never thought in a million years he would ever touch, let alone wear the shoes Mr. Smith cared so deeply about. With that thought, Jacob jumped up and said to Mr. Smith, "my life has been to make you proud. Thank you for <u>seeing me for who I am and could be and not for who I was</u>." They cried and hugged. As Jacob got dressed, he noticed Mr. Smith struggling to stay on his feet. He turned his back out of respect because he knew Mr. Smith was a proud man who will keep his dignity no matter what. And he knew he did not want to see his hero in that predicament. As they finish dressing, they both walk to the big Hall that was in the middle of town. Many had seen this building but few had ever been inside and the few that did were sworn to secrecy.

Now, mind you, this era still had lots of racism and class Warfare. So for blacks to own a hall and it was not a dump but instead, being something that even the whites rented out says a lot about the blacks that owned the hall. This Hall had three different floors and they all had different functions going at the same time. On this night, the blacks had the third floor; the second floor was for a white doctor convention that was going on at the same time and the first floor was hosting a wedding for Miss Pearl, the librarian at the school who was marrying Ted who works in maintenance. The basement was a mystery as no one had ever been down there and those who did would never admit to the goings-on there. There was a parlor on the first floor that all floors could gather for a smoke and a drink or just to sit there and wet their social whistle. Mr. Smith and Mr. Jacob arrived at the hall; they were led to the third floor by a butler. As Mr. Smith and Jacob followed the butler up the stairs. Mr. Smith stumbled almost falling back down the stairs but Jacob caught him just in time helping him regain his balance. Mr. Smith looked Jacob in the face and said go on, it's your night don't let me slow you down, I just lost my balance. That's all he said smiling as he pushed Jacob forward. Mr. Jacobs said, "old man, even if it takes all night, we will get there together. They walked shoulder to shoulder into the banquet room arriving to standing ovations. Mr. Jacob was overwhelmed; he could not believe so many prominent African-Americans existed. He also saw whites in the crowd as well which was a shock because usually, they only show up to the lectures in small towns so as not to be seen commingling with the blacks. So for whites to be seen in the city mingling with blacks was definitely out of the ordinary. Before a word could be spoken, Mr. Jacob turned to Mr. Smith and said, "without you guiding me, I would have never made it to this place. How glorious it is God saw fit to have you walk across the threshold with me still by your side the same as the day I met you. You are here with me but it is I who shall forever be singing your praises in the highest order." As the meeting came to order, the first piece of business was for the honoree to deliver the opening address. Mr. Jacob was to receive the black Excellence award for all he did for his fellow African-Americans. Mr. Jacob accepted his award then gave a speech on why it was so important to him to teach and reach as many people as he could. He explained the importance of Intellectual development and how it transitioned him out of a world he felt lost in and Into a new one where he had a purpose. He talked about how life will set out to destroy you if you let it. *There will always be things that can take you off the path of excellence. In your mind, you must hold fast to your final destination in life. Your goals and purpose must outweigh any inclination that you will not make it. He said if you wake up every day determined to be a success, then eventually, you will find your way there. With dedication and a little elbow grease, nothing is impossible. He spoke on the importance of Outlook; He said a man will only see as far as the trees. He said the trees represent the boundaries they have programmed into their minds. With a book, the horizon becomes endless as one learns to no longer focus on the trees that once-obscured one's sight but instead one decide to look past them. Keep on walking he said. Walk until the thing that once blocked your path as a barrier is now the thing that keeps you from going back to who you used to be. Forever chase who you are supposed to become. He said, "in order to see the true possibilities for our lives we first must cut down the barriers that blocked the road to progression then plant flowers of freedom along the path for others to follow along. Let us contemplate a better understanding of peace while we gaze upon the wings of knowledge that come to feed there."*

Mr. Jacobs believed that no man or woman with a very strong determination and willpower plus tenacity could ever be held back from achieving all that they set out to do. He continued to talk at length about the importance of character. He believes it's the principles you stand on that determine the height of your achievements. As he was speaking, he could see a commotion in the back, nothing alarming at that moment. But it became a concern rather fast because of the commotion that seemed to be surrounding where Mr. Smith had been sitting. Mr. Jacobs continued to talk at length about the endless possibilities that character provides. As he spoke, every second seemed like an eternity as his eyes remained locked on the small crowd that had started to disperse. Upon the crowd clearing out, he noticed his teacher was no longer sitting in his chair. He finished his speech quickly and began to make his way towards the exit; the only thing on his mind was Mr. Smith. Due to his magnificent speech, he was called back to the stage to give a toast in his honor. He graciously took the stage, trying to hide his worry and anxiety under the smile he painted on. Upon finishing the toast Mr. Jacobs moved quickly towards the door smiling, shaking hands, and getting pats on the back but he never lost his stride. Once he made it out to the main hall, he was greeted by a server who asked, "Are you looking for that gentleman you came in with?" Yes sir, he explained in a bold tone. He asked where he is? and why has he gone?. "Has something happened to him?" The server responded, "calm yourself. I'm sure he is safe. Why don't you make your way to the Parlor? There are bound to be some answers there." Jacob thanked the server feverishly as he hurried along to the Parlor and began asking about his teacher. It felt like the more he asked, the more he hit a wall. It felt like no one knew where he was as if Mr. Smith never existed. The bartender overhearing him ask about his teacher called him over to the bar; he asked, "

Are you looking for that fella that was in the meeting on the third floor?" " Yes," Jacob yelled excitedly. "Where is he? Please tell me now." The bartender said, "there is a match next to the fireplace. Seek the Candlestick and light it and only then shall you brighten your way." "It didn't make sense," Mr. Jacobs proclaimed. "Sir I don't have time to figure out riddles, where is he? I need to find him, please help me." The bartender responded, "knowledge only came by the way of Enlightenment; so, light one must have to maintain a proper path." Jacob became frustrated with the bartender and he quickly retreated, deciding against prodding him for any more information. Becoming frustrated with nothing else to lose, he decided to light the candle. So he struck a match and pulled the Candlestick down to light it and at that moment, the fireplace instantaneously rotated around and he found himself in another room that was exactly adjacent to the Parlor. It was a library of sorts and the books seemed to go on forever. He was shocked at the length of the rows of books. He imagined that someone had gone through a lot to collect all the books contained in this room. He was quickly taken off task at the sight of such vast amounts of knowledge. He never even imagined that this many books even existed. So to see it with his own eyes was overwhelming, to say the least.

Remembering his true reason for this occasion, he quickly regained focus and began to talk to the men who littered the room debating the many different conundrums of life. He quickly infiltrated the groups asking about his friend with no luck until he got to one group of gentlemen standing around a pit of fire. The pit had a long beam that led to the middle of the fire and it had writing that said, "Only the truly righteous should ever try to walk here for the foolish shall surely perish." As the men were talking, Jacob walked up to them and asked, "Have you seen my teacher? one man responded, "look at the fire, it cleans all infirmities." Not understanding what he was told, he concluded that maybe they just wanted to see him burn himself for their delight. He figured his teacher was burned alive and began to sob uncontrollably; then he felt a hand on his shoulder. He turned and it was the server and he told him to gather control of himself. The road to truth is made pure in the light because the fire shall burn away all that is foul and unclean. He pointed at the fire and said now go and face your destiny. Mr. Jacobs looked at the pit and with tears rolling down his face soaking his shirt, he began to walk towards the pit. Suddenly, the room fell silent; the men retreating from all formalities parted ways, watching curiously as Mr. Jacobs slowly and softly walked towards the fire that seemed to gather in intensity with every step. They all stare intently at this man who seemed to be walking towards his imminent death. Jacob stopped as he got close as fear paralyzed his body but he felt the waiter behind him encouraging him with a nudge to go on and face his destiny. As he turned and looked; he realized that the men had enclosed around him and there was no way to retreat. The waiter proclaimed he will only find his truth in the flame for the fire shall light his way. He gazed in the direction as the long arm pointing from behind him aimed pinpoint on the fire. He looks back at the warm smile on the waiter's face then turns to walk towards the plank. In the heat of the flames is where the answers to your questions can be found. As the waiter pointed Mr. Jacob to the plank. Mr. Jacob stepped out on the plank and started to walk toward the center. As he walked into the middle of the flames, they blazed in intensity letting off an invasive heat causing all who stood close to look away. Just as the flames roared hotter the plank held, Mr.

Jacobs began to cry out in horror at the fate he felt awaiting him as he gazed upon the silhouettes of people he could see through the flames. With a crack, the plank gave way as if on a lever and Mr. Jacob disappeared in the flames in a blink of an eye. Only a final horrific yell was proof that he actually existed and just like that, he was gone or so it might have seemed to all who were in the room.

He landed on his back looking up at the center of the pit floor closing above him. To all who look from the outside, it seemed that Mr. Jacob had just committed suicide. Some could not believe what they had just seen but most felt it was a good lesson for a boy who asked too many questions. There were a lot of mixed feelings in the room although none would display their true emotion to the situation. They held back their emotions with all trying to remain more stoic than the next for the fear of being thought of as inferior in this game of emotional charades. They continue to talk in the library of sorts, having drinks and smoking their cigars trying to look courageous in the face of so many scrutinizing eyes that seemed to examine each other like a surgeon ready to pinpoint any area of weakness present. The suspense in the room was heavy, the air thick and smokey almost burning your eyes. The smell of mahogany lay in the air gently mingling with the cigar smoke, producing an almost intoxicatingly overstimulating sniff of the male persona. And this only gave a testament to the men in the room because after all, we are talking about some of the brightest, most accomplished men of their time. And you better believe that they will live up to the stuffed shirt, obnoxious insensitive demeaning a sometimes cruel show of bigotry the elite are known for. I mean not all were this way but a good majority of the room was. So if you felt different, it would be best if you kept your little minority mouth closed if you knew what's best for you. People are always quick to yell secrecy and loyalty until they feel hurt by you. Or if they decide to attack you for your livelihood because you are more successful than them. It is in moments like these that you will find all bets are off and you somehow get exposed through writings in the clouds. So it would be best you keep your composure and hold on to your reputation one and the same. Some in there knew what lay beneath but were sworn to secrecy and the secret was never revealed. Mr. Jacobs was in shock at what he witnessed once he had gathered his bearings.

When he stood up, he could not believe what he saw. It was a makeshift hospital with a very foul odor. By the standards of what he was used to seeing, it was way cleaner than the average slave house but still a very foul place to be. Now, it was starting to make sense why this town hall was able to exist in the middle of the town and no one ever did a thing to it even though it was black-owned. You see, it caters to the affluent and their sick families. It was a place the upper class could put their sick and know they would get the best care possible. No one ever lived to tell about their stay there and no one visited out of fear of contracting the plague. It was very primitive but still a functioning ward located in what was in reality a small dank cellar underneath the hall. The freshly dead and dying were housed in the same area due to the small amount of space. There were whites and blacks down there. Although segregation existed outside the walls, inside they all remained in the same room. They did try to remain as separate as possible.

Mr. Jacobs immediately found Mr. Smith and they began to weep together. Mr. Smith begged Mr. Jacobs to go. He said, "leave me for what I have, There is no cure now, go before it's too late and you suffer the same fate as me." Mr. Jacobs responded. "I will never leave you, for when I was low, you raised me up. When I was lonely, you comforted me. Where I was dumb, you taught me. I owe you my life. I shall never leave you. We will leave here together; you will be alright. I promise I won't let you die; I will save you," proclaimed Mr. Jacob boldly. Mr. Smith began to beg as tears rolled down his face for Mr. Jacobs to go as there was no hope. "I believe there is a cure," Mr. Jacob said, rubbing Mr. Smith's head and holding his hand to comfort him. Mr. Jacob added, "I believe there is a cure and I will find it, or we shall die together. But no matter the outcome, I shall never leave your side." By this time, the other sick white people and their caretakers were becoming increasingly vexed at Jacob's attempt to comfort Mr. Smith with such flagrant statements. So the caretakers and the families of the sick that gave up their lives to stay down there became viciously angry. They began to yell obscenities as they attempted to lecture and educate what they thought were two dumb niggas. They demanded Mr. Jacobs answer questions like, "Do you not have any sense of compassion? You sit and tell a sick man he shall be well when you know surely as we sit that he shall perish. What gives you the right to spout such nonsense?" Before Mr. Jacobs could respond, he was knocked to the floor with a vicious head blow. When he looked up, he was surrounded by four white guys who were there to help the sick whites and to also prevent the family members who decided to stay down there from escaping. They ask Jacob why they should not take him outside and hang him right now. You should have known better than to come here with your foolish talk. Mr. Jacob proclaimed, "I can do it sir, I swear I can do it; just give me a chance." Before Mr. Jacobs could say another word, one of the men began to choke him violently, thrashing him about as the others spit on him and called him names.

As Mr. Jacobs began to lose consciousness, Mr. Smith tried to speak up for Mr. Jacobs in what weak voice he had left. But before Mr. Smith could finish his words, the men yelled, "Shut up or we will take you out back and burn you alive next to this boy we are going to hang." Mr. Smith crawled out of bed hitting the floor with a loud thud as he dragged his weak body over to the men that were assaulting Mr. Jacob. Before Mr. Smith could get close to Mr.

Jacobs, one of the men would drag him by his legs across the hard concrete floor and throw him in a corner. It says a lot when men think so low of you that they don't consider you human enough to beat anymore and instead of beating you, they throw you in the corner like a piece of trash. Mr. Smith would have his belly skin scraped until the pink flesh was showing and his chest scraped raw and bleeding before this incident would be over. But Mr. Smith wouldn't stop; every time they pulled him back, he would start crawling again. Even with the threat of death, he continued to crawl towards Mr. Jacobs scraping his torso and hands all while pleading for Jacob. He grabbed hold of one of the men's legs and wouldn't let go no matter how many times he was kicked and punched. He continued to plead for Mr. Jacobs. Due to Mr. Smith's persistence, the man loosened his grip as Mr. Jacobs gasped for air, tears streaming down his face as he stood shaking, his feet barely touching the ground. He stood in terror wondering if the man closed his hands again, would he still be alive when he opened them back up again. Before Mr. Jacobs could catch his breath, he was already being interrogated again. They ask Mr. Jacobs, "Where did you get them clothes and who gave a dumb nigger like you some shoes like that? No nigger deserves shoes better than a white man, take them off the white man ordered." Jacob began to plead but with every word, he was struck in the face and all around his head until blood poured from the wounds hatred once again decided to inflict on him. *"Lord, I wonder, is it too much to save a man as just as these men? Just this once, could You come down and intervene? I know we are meant to walk our path but I wonder if this is too much for these men to bear. I only ask because I can barely stand to write anymore. Can you please stop this? I can't stand to watch this movie in my mind anymore. I understand I must write what I see, so I shall finish the job through tears because I can't stop what I'm seeing. Please excuse the over-emotional side of my humanity. They only saw shiny shoes but those shoes meant much more to them."* He pleaded for the shoes relentlessly. He begged them, "don't take my shoes," tears running down his face as he crouched in a ball holding his shoes with an unbreakable grip. That's when they started beating him with sticks and threatening to kill him if he didn't comply with their demands. They beat him brutally then stripped him naked and dragged him by his arms across the course concrete floor to a chalkboard across the room. They pointed at it and said, "you see here, this is white man's work; it's probably too smart for your dumb nigger brain to comprehend." Mr. Jacobs understood every word on that board but dared not say anything that would incite them to beat him more or maybe even take his life. He looked at them and said, "I'm sorry sir, please let me live and I will clean and care for all who are here. I will never say anything about getting well again I promise. Let me live and stay. I will serve you all. I will be the best caretaker you have ever seen." They looked at each other and smiled; then they beat him some more. They beat him until he lay moaning in his urine and feces. His body was brutalized beyond imagination and yet after all that he endured, they found pleasure in dressing him in some Rags they got off one of the men that had died that day. They forced him to put the clothes on. They told him a dead man doesn't deserve nice clothes because he will be dead soon anyway. He put on the smelly clothes soaked with body odor and fluids and was made to empty the bedpans under the beds and cleanse the room of soiled bandages. Mr. Jacobs did this for the next 4 years.

The doctor would come once a month and he would always study the board to see what he was prescribing. One day Mr. Jacobs asked the doctor how he decided the best methods to treat patients and the doctor pointed to a Shelf with three rows of books. The doctor pointed to a book that was on the top shelf second from the left and he said, "you see, that book, that's where I am. I am positive the answer lies in one of those books somewhere. I just have to find it but I only have so much time because there are so many sick people to help, so I read what I can. Mr. Jacobs had developed his plan of action within seconds of hearing the doctor's method for treating his patients. His first order of business was to clean the facility as clean as possible. But as time continued to pass, somehow, word got out through a cloud maybe but word began to travel about how Mr. Jacobs and Mr. Smith were being treated and outrage became rampant across the towns. The blacks would voice their outrage to the owner everywhere he went. Soon, the sheriff came in and declared Mr. Jacobs and Mr. Smith untouchable. He proclaimed anyone who dared to so much as bump his chair while walking by him would be put to death immediately. What they didn't know is the sheriff's daughter-in-law died there eight years prior, so he knew of that place and he also knew the doctor who visited there and how he talked very highly of Jacob and his potential. Dr. Sterlingzinger was still sending him money by the way which he used for supplies every month. Mr. Jacob sent Dr. Sterlingzinger a request for one of the old units that he maybe did not need as it would be a big help at the facility. The doctor sent back a postcard with the words in bold letters **Never**. Jacob didn't know how to take it. His heart sank with tears in his eyes; he began to tell Mr. Smith what the postcard said. Mr. Smith asked Mr. Jacobs, "What are you crying about?" Mr. Jacobs replied, "I'm trying so hard, but at every turn, I am being set back. I don't know what to do. I know I can't give up, but I don't think I got what it takes to help you. I tried everything I knew," he said, sobbing profusely. Mr. Smith looked at Jacob and said, "I have faith in you son. I have never seen you fail at anything you set your mind to. I know you will get it done; so stand up, wipe your face and let's move on to the next order of business." Mr. Jacobs grabbed a book off the shelf and began to read; about a week later, he finished the first book. He continued to care for patients, feeding and changing them and studying in between. One day, a servant came downstairs yelling, "Mr. Jacob, come here right away." Mr. Jacobs began to shake with anxiety and terror as he did not know what all the commotion could be about. They yelled, "come with me, come now let's go; hurry up as they pulled Mr. Jacobs along to the staircase in the back of the cellar that led to a long hallway and some stairs to the yard outback. They shuffled him hurriedly up the stairs to the window. When he reached the window, he could see a delivery had been made right outside the door to the basement. He knew what it was as soon as he saw it. It was a brand-new sterilizing unit with the words; "you saw my dream through; now I shall see yours come to pass, never shall I ever send you something second class for you are first class in my eyes and only deserve the best." Mr. Jacobs began to cry and dance for joy. The servants and family members as well as the sick in the basement began to cry because Mr. Jacobs had been taking care of them for many years and they all felt he was due for a blessing. He never asked for anything from anyone; so when he got this machine, everyone celebrated it because he truly deserved it and so much more.

The unit was installed immediately and the conditions, as well as the morale around the place, began to improve almost immediately. To say the unit gave the patient true hope would be an understatement. I think they thought if he, being a black man, could obtain such a piece of equipment, then maybe he might be able to help them get better after all. Looking back at the way he was treated in his youth might lead some to wonder if maybe he was just misunderstood from the beginning. I don't think he magically became great. I think this great man came from a confused little boy with no future to look forward to. Maybe, what those white men perceived as arrogant was just Mr. Jacob's true ability. Shining through it was the helper in him and nothing more. He would not and could not stop helping others even if his life depended on it. He became very well respected and greatly appreciated around the facility. The same people that once tormented him to no avail now wait on him hand and foot, making light work of any request that he might have. For the first time, they had hot water, heat, and clean bandages. What once was a dark-rank basement now becomes clean and orderly.

Mr. Jacobs worked in this basement for a total of 7 years and at the end of the seventh year, he had read all of the books on the shelf. He had slowed down the rate of death in his makeshift facility until he eventually stopped it. It used to be people dying every day but while Mr. Jacobs was there, it dropped to one patient every 3 months then to none. Mr. Smith was still alive, his condition improved from very near death to bed-bound. Mr. Jacobs had seemed to hit a plateau as it seems his patients stopped improving any further. It was like once the patients reached the stage of not healing but not getting any worse, they seemed to no longer show any signs of further Improvement. This situation seems to perplex Mr. Jacobs to no end. He feverishly studied his notes day and night and still could not find the error or defect in his methods. He was completely dumbfounded as to what was the cause of the plateau. In his frustration, he studied non-stop as he felt he was close but just couldn't figure out what was causing the plateau effect. He fell into a quick sleep at his desk and had a dream of walking through the market and seeing many different varieties of fruit. He could smell and touch each one but could not taste them. He awoke more tired than before he napped and was confused about his dream but yet, he pondered its meaning. He couldn't understand the concept of the fruit and what it could mean. It was just a useless fruit and a weird dream. So <u>he tried to disregard the dream but it would not go away.</u> He went on with his daily agenda and at noon, sat to have lunch. Some of the food he ate was sent to his Chambers via the townspeople as well.

Some of the townspeople knew about the hidden facility but never got to enter it but had family who died there. So they would never reveal its entrance let alone its existence. The facility was shrouded in secrecy because hatred and racism were alive and ever-present; so it needed to remain concealed under the cover of darkness if you will. Let's not forget that this hall was in the center of town and owned by an educated black man. Then you have a black man (Mr. Jacobs) in a makeshift clinic that thinks he is a doctor and can do what the white doctors can't. This would be considered blasphemy in the highest order and would almost ensure without a doubt hanging by the neck until dead in the town square.

Mr. Jacob was a teacher without ever knowing it. His wise teaching was always being talked about from town to town; he had become a living legend, almost the object that folklore could be founded on. I mean a slave hand from a field that became a Doctor. A black man that could read as well as manufacture effective treatments. For the people of that time, this sounded like a fictional character almost like the saying, "they were kings in their own land long ago." Kind of like the old negro spiritual wade in the water and this little light of mine. I remember hearing songs like this and thought it's an old church song; the old black churches loved to sing about our past.

As I grew mentally, I began to understand the meaning of these songs. I also learned the true intentions of why some of these songs were created. I think the intention was to give others hope and to also spread the word in code if you will kind of like a morse code. I am sure a lot of the blacks who heard of Mr. Jacobs never thought that one day this could happen in reality. They probably could never even imagine that the story was true. But the truth is that he was alive and treating whites and blacks as well. Mr. Jacobs sat in agony as he pondered the dream and the dilemma that he finds himself in. As he pondered his dream, lunch was brought in to him and as he sat down to eat; he looked at the plate and noticed a jam on the side of his plate with two slices of bread. He inquired about the jam as he normally would not receive such a treat. preserves and jams were a sign of status. He asked where it came from and the servant told him that a white woman whose son was seriously ill with pneumonia was cured with one of his medications and she sent the preserve to say thank you. The server replied, "I hear it's a mixed fruit version and many consider it some of the best in the land. It's expensive and in short supply; you must be truly extraordinary to receive such a gift. I have seen this type of jam and never had the honor of tasting such a delicacy. At that moment, Jacob jumped up proclaiming "I've got it;" his eyes stretched to their widest ever. The server stood there in shock as if he saw a ghost with a blank look covering his face. Mr. Jacob continued to jump and scream; "I got it, I think I figured it. I know what the fruit means," he proclaimed as he hugged the waiter. The waiter, not knowing what to make of the whole thing just looked confused as he thought he was talking about the jam that he just brought him on his plate. "The waiter saw jelly, but to me, it was my answer to the conundrum that has left me imprisoned in my thoughts and constantly perplexed. I think I can cure the disease," he said as he was running, jumping, and dancing. He and the server both begin crying and dancing in celebratory fashion. Mr. Jacobs ran to Mr. Smith's bedside, tears rolling down his face saying, "get your walking shoes ready because we will walk out of here together." With raw emotion and sincerity, he looked Mr. Jacobs in the face and said, "*I never once doubted you. I knew you could figure it all out. I always knew you were a valuable piece of land and if I tilled your soil just right, you would grow out of mediocrity to heights I could only have hoped to conquer. I was provided the same opportunity by my teacher Mr. Williams and I gave you the same dedication that was given me. Your soil contains the knowledge, sweat, and blessing of me and my teacher and the other great men you met along the way. Let these blessings be the nourishment to the mental wounds that were inflicted on our people by this so-called free man society they tell us we are in. They will talk about you in many towns all over. You will give our people hope; you will give us a standard to strive towards. You are our moment in the sun and I am so happy you shone on me.*" At that moment Mr. Jacobs jumped on the bed and hugged Mr. Smith so tight that he could barely breathe. Jacob whispered back to Mr. Smith and said, "it was you that gave me hope." And at that moment, Mr. Smith held him tight and proclaimed, "my son, I have never been more honored than the day I met you. Through you, I saw me. I saw my chance to give you what my teacher gave me, <u>hope.</u>" As Jacob kissed his cheek, he said, "you gave me more than that. You have been my role model, teacher, and leader, but most of all, you are my friend. You gave me a new beginning and I shall forever be indebted to you." Mr. Jacobs began explaining his dream to Mr. smith. He said, "I had a dream. I was walking through the market and it was filled with endless fruit of all different varieties and flavors; then I awoke. I knew the dream had significant meaning but it made no sense to me or so I thought at the time. I pondered it all morning to no avail. I just couldn't figure it out. Then for lunch today, I was given a marvelous jam." He motioned for the server to retrieve it with the bread as well. Upon the servant's return, he spread the jam on the bread and they took a piece and ate. Mr.

Smith, not understanding, replied, "I still don't understand; what does this mean Jacob? With a smile, Mr. Jacob made a slice of bread smeared with the fruit Jam for the servant. Mr. Smith was still confused; Jacob sensing his frustration started to chuckle out loud. "Allow me to explain this to you old man," as he smiles with a warm majestic glow on his face. He said, *"the fruit represents the endless Sea of available medications. On their own, they are effective but limited in their action, but mixed, they become something so much more. He added, "I understand now why we have reached the plateau. It's because our body has become regulated to the one medication; so the only way to continue the healing process is that we must tweak the medication. By adding other medications at set intervals, we can keep the body from becoming accustomed to the original set of medications. So instead of plateauing, the body will continue to improve as it must consistently adapt to different combinations all geared towards improving one's overall condition. Why should one settle for apples and cherries each being good on their own but combined give an amazing new flavor? This is what combining the medications can do for you all."* With this vision, the beginnings of combination medication therapy were being thought into existence at that very moment. <u>Led by his dream, he started working immediately</u> on the different combinations that could be used and would be effective within a short period. Not only did he find the cure, he also created a whole new line of drugs that were multi-effective.

CHAPTER NINE

In the seventh month of the ninth year, Mr. Smith and Mr. Jacob walked out of the basement full of health and energy. Mr. Jacobs never got sick with so much as a cold while he stayed in the basement with the many sick that came and died there. He credited this to the few years he spent with doctor Sterlingzinger. The day that Jacob was set to walk out of the basement, he received a package. It just said, "Mr. Jacobs," in big letters. Both Mr. Jacobs and Mr. Smith received a package, upon opening it, they each found new shoes that fit perfectly as if they were made especially for them. Mr. Smith opened his first; inside were a beautiful pair of black highly polished dress shoes with solid gold tips on the trim. Mr. Smith didn't know whether to wear them or hide them for he had never seen such a glorious pair of shoes. Mr. Jacobs looked on, smiling at Mr. Smith, and just then, Mr. Smith looked at Jacob and said, "Aren't you going to open it?" Mr. Jacobs picked up the package and unwrapped it as carefully and delicately as possible. Under the paper were the shoes that were beaten off of him and taken upon his arrival to the basement. Mr. Jacobs and Mr. Smith cried tears of joy because he thought those shoes were gone forever never to be seen again but there they were, shiny and black looking just as new as the day he took them off. They left that place looking as good as they did before their journey through sickness. They looked even better, just a couple of days older I like to think.

After they walked out of there, the very next morning, they walked right back into the facility again but this time, not as prisoners to circumstance but as a doctor and a teacher. They cleaned and painted the basement and created the first walk-in clinic. Using the same door, they would carry the dead out in the back. All who needed help could enter the facility to see Mr. Smith and Jacob. The word of the two successes spread far and wide. word traveled so far that it had made it up North. The word was that there was a rural clinic that was doing the impossible and soon people came from far and wide to get healing for their infirmities but to also learn the most cutting-edge procedures around. Doctor Sterlingzinger hearing all the good news sent his best wishes and in return, he got an invitation to become the head of the facility, teaching his techniques and procedures on infection control and proper tool sterilization which he agreed to happily.

The three Men became the head of the first medically designated facility ever created. The facility procedures and medications were so up-to-date that other areas would send their big-city doctors with all their education to a rule town to learn applications of theory from two former field workers and a medical doctor who was considered a fool by most of his counterparts for a long time. **Time will always tell the truth even when the world tries to hide your true intentions.** Our character will always show the world who we truly are. So you can always pretend to be someone else but when playtime is over, you will still be stuck with the same old you. So change and be free to fly, or lie and remain caged. The truth will always come out no matter how deep you try to bury it. Wait no longer to live your dreams because your purpose is too important to leave to chance.

The End

Conclusion

When I first started writing this book, I had no idea it would morph into the magnificent story that lay before you. Of this, I am proud. I have just finished a book that took so much emotion to write. I like to think of myself as a tough guy but to be honest, the tears flowed heavily as I wrote pieces of this book. For me, I felt as if I was right there as a silent onlooker to the scenes of torment that played on the screen in my subconscious theater. I must admit I'm crying now. I'm just in awe at the things a man can achieve if he would just put his mind to it and leave it there. To watch human suffering is something I hope no one ever has to see, but honestly, we see it every day, especially me as a nurse by profession.

This book I hope will make you think more. I hope it makes you want to dream more and strive to be more than you were yesterday. I want you to know that life has some amazing journeys to take you on, but first, you must believe you deserve such things. I have seen so many people with dreams die before they come to pass. Life is a journey but it can end at any moment; so I implore you to put your plan to action because tomorrow for you may never come. One thing I have grown to understand is that life on earth is very short compared to the longevity of death. I want you to realize that you will have an eternity to think about the short time you had to enjoy this place called earth. So stand up, get off your ass and chase your dreams because, God forbid, He takes you before you ever find out just how special you are. I believe in you but I think the real question is, what do you believe about yourself? Are you what your immediate surroundings call you? Are you the raggedy house, the debt, or the habit or are you so much more? I want you to decide for yourself who you are because only you know.

Don't listen to the world because they said you can't be anything; listen to your heart because it will tell you who you truly are. I know you have had negative experiences in your life but haven't we all? Even the greatest men had to go through some adversity; so why shouldn't you? I want to tell you that the difference between the winners in life and the losers is that when the troubles came to destroy you, the looser stopped and said, "it's too much." But the winner said, "it's too much, but yet, I shall press on." There is a saying that whatever doesn't kill you only makes you stronger. I would rather say, "whatever you go through will only make you more ferocious and more capable of destroying the next task that decides to show its face." Adversity will never kill a man but it is the quickest way to reveal who that man truly is and what he is made of. Lots of people will tell you they are great but when trouble comes, you will see how great they truly are. The fact of the matter is that most people fold and give up at the beginning and they rest before they get to the finish line. Stand tall and see your dream through; you are more than you could ever imagine. I know you are great but do you? I refuse to be lied to by the world and the small community of people and situations that I am accustomed to dictating my existence.

Turn your head from your past and move to your destiny because greatness is waiting for you. I want to stress, even yell it into your mind until it sinks into your soul that you have a purpose. I don't care what life has thrown at you; it doesn't matter your situation; the only thing that matters is how you overcame them and didn't let them overcome you.

Next, I want to address how you talk to yourself. **Never again call your shortcomings out but focus on your greatness and vow to attack every situation that life throws your way. The only shortcoming you have is a lack of discipline; get your head on right and I promise you will accomplish more than you ever could have imagined**. Program your mind with the thought that you will either destroy your shortcomings or conquer them to the point that they never affect you negatively again. **When you decide to be great, then life will start to make a path for you but you must first seek this path to find it.**

Decide today whom you want to become and once you decide, spend every day working towards the person you know you are meant to be. This book was written by divine inspiration and it was written for you. If you were looking for a sign to tell you to pick your head up and move forward, then look in your hand because that's exactly what this is. Now, let me give you my take on the meaning of certain things I found very significant in this story. I am reading this for the first time as you are. The story is fictional but the message is as real as you and me.

The shoes

The shoes represented pride in oneself. Those shoes came with a story. They had a bloody background but continue to shine on. We all have had many things go wrong in our lives that make us want to quit and give up on life but I want you to conjure up this one thing and that is pride in yourself. You are the only one holding you back. **I promise there will be no rescue party sent for you. You are your rescue**. Sit for a minute and look inside yourself and listen to that inner voice that tells you all the right things to do. That is your guide and it has been waiting to lead you to the peace you desire. If you're like me, you have searched everywhere on your own and have not found your true calling or destiny if you will. I want to tell you that all the answers to your problems are in you and always have been. Wherever you find yourself is because you thought your way there and the only way out is taking pride in yourself to say not me, not anymore; I'm getting out of here; I can do better than this. But it first must start with you. Mr. Williams' dad had pride in who he was and who he could become. He knew farming was not his family's lot in life. Being a poor field hand was not all he was; he decided to be so much more. I know you see Mr. Williams' dad's death as a sad incident and it truly was but I also want you to understand that through his death, he gave Mr. Williams a reason for living. But most of all, his death gave Williams a pride that no matter how bad it got, he would finish the task his father never got to complete. The pride that exuded from Mr. Williams was instilled in the little almost deaf boy from the farm that could barely hear or speak. And the same pride that was instilled in Mr. Smith was also passed to Jacob and look what they became. You must trust yourself and not your feelings because your emotions are a lie and when they say stop, give up or quit, you beat those thoughts to the ground and tell them, "I'll never quit on my dreams again because I'm worth seeing all that I can become."

We all know what we must do with our lives but we allow our emotions to guide our decisions when this should never be the case. Make the change no matter how hard it is because you love yourself. One must develop a sense of Pride about oneself that you are special, you are unique and you are created for a reason. But first, you must understand that no one will ever think this way about you unless you first think this way about yourself. So if you are low on self-esteem, put your pride on like you put on your shoes and start to walk proud, talk proud, treat yourself proud until it becomes a part of you. When you start to Value yourself, the world will start to take notice of just how valuable you truly are. Every day, put your pride on and don't take it off, and if it wears out, then put on a whole new suit each morning because your life is valuable and you are worth more than you could even begin to imagine.

The characters

Mr. Williams :

This character pointed out that sometimes life is hard and it is for many people for many different reasons. When I think of what he witnessed as a child, I think how so many who went through what he went through gave up on life. They became drunks and drug addicts or people who just gave up on life. But could you blame them or fault them after they told you their story? In all honesty, you would probably feel sorry for him and tell him it's ok; he had a hard childhood. But Mr. Williams didn't take that route; he did not take the easy way out. He decided that he would fight to be everything his father wanted to be but never had the chance to become. He could have given up on life but instead, he decided to fight. He was not going to take the easy route and come up with a bunch of reasons why he couldn't make it or why he didn't try. No, he took the same pride, the same tenacity that they killed his father for and he turned that tragedy into triumph. He took what would have destroyed most and used it to propel him forward and because of this attitude, he went on to teach hundreds more, maybe even thousands more how to live with pride and to be a person of dignity. I want you to always remember this poor farm boy who saw his daddy killed in front of him at a young age and went on to be a great teacher to many. He had a lot of setbacks growing up in those times but yet, he made it. So tell me, what is your excuse? Now I don't mean to come off as disrespectful in any way but I just want you to understand how imperative it is that we no longer use these tragedies as the reason for us not to get up and try anymore. I understand what happened to you was hard but I also want you to understand that you are so much more than your circumstances.

Sometimes our circumstances happen to teach us something we may not understand at that moment but hopefully, in the future, it is revealed to you the reason why you had to suffer the way you did. When I think about what Mr. Williams had to go through, I think about how he used it to give him a reason to live. So even if you never find out the reason why such things happened to you, maybe you can turn it around and use it as a reason to live. Use it as a reason to make sure that you fight every day that it doesn't happen to somebody else because you know what it felt like because it happened to you. It doesn't matter if nobody believed it happened to you. **I believe you.** Now go out and change the world and make it a better place because, without people like you, it'll keep on happening. **Mr. Williams gave you the perfect example of what we are supposed to do with our pain. We are never supposed to let our pain stop us but we are supposed to use it as fuel to help propel us. We are to use it as the reason why we will never stop climbing but we are never to use it as a reason for why we never climbed.**

MR JACOBS

When I think about Mr. Jacobs, I think about a man who was so smart as a kid but just in the wrong environment. You can become so great in life. But one must make sure to constantly search out the environments that help us to become great. You can be so great but if you're not in the place where your greatness is received, you will go unnoticed. I've seen so many talented people who just couldn't find where they belong, so they gave up and became part of the masses. I don't want you to ever give up on your dream. I don't want you to ever give up on being an individual. We all have our shortcomings. You know I'm pretty sure they told him how dumb he was and how he would never amount to anything. I'm pretty sure he heard it a lot. He was probably picked on and laughed at and belittled but yet, he continued to dream. He didn't let his surroundings be his end all and be all. What others saw as their ending, he saw as his beginning beyond the fence. I bet if he told anybody about his dreams or that he thought about going past the fence, they probably would have told him to shut up. I can hear them now saying, "close your mouth, you're too stupid to ever leave this place. If I ain't leaving, you ain't going to get out of here because I'm smarter than you." I know you heard this line from the losers around you or was it just me? But you know what, he knew where he was going. He knew what was in his heart; so he continued to dream until he finally met Mr. Smith. When he saw Mr. Smith, he saw his opportunity to escape where he was and to finally go where he knew he belonged. You see the funny thing in life is perception is everything. In Mr. Williams' case, most people only saw tragedy, but he saw a reason for triumph. Mr. Jacobs saw a fence that kept him confined for a moment. Where others accepted their situation, Mr. Jacob saw a future that had no fence to keep his dreams subdued. So I think the most important question is, "When you look at your life, do you see what everybody else sees for your life, or do you believe what that voice deep down inside is telling you to become?" You can tell me you believe what that voice inside you says. But I will say, "What does your surroundings show? ' This will be the lead indicator of exactly what you have been thinking. You are so much more and you're meant to do amazing things if only you had more faith in yourself. Do you have faith in yourself? I think you're the only one that can answer this question because deep down inside, you're the only one who knows who you truly are. I say, all the people that doubt you and tell you that you will never amount to anything haven't a clue of how valuable you truly are and in time, you will prove them all wrong. But first, I need you to prove me right. I know I'm right about you; there's something great in you; something amazing is buried deep inside you and I just need you to search until you find it. When you find it, live your life enjoying the real you to the fullest because when you're old and gray and sitting in your recliner in your room, the only person you will have to fault for not going after your dreams is you. Don't regret not ever going after your dreams. If anything, regret that you didn't go after every one of them and complete them all before your time was out. I want you to always remember that you are full of life and when you die, make sure you die empty.

MR SMITH

To me, Mr. Smith represents everybody that suffers from some sort of shortcoming. Whether the shortcoming is physical, mental or emotional, it is still a burden no matter the form it presents itself in. Mr. Smith had the kind of shortcomings that would almost guarantee him a pitiful existence in those times. In all actuality, he's lucky to be alive. You see, because of his shortcomings, he was written off as a young child. He was already considered useless from the day he was born. Now I know some of you can relate to that because I can. I didn't grow up with a family that loved me unconditionally. I grew up with a family that made sure to tell me at every chance they got that I would never amount to anything. For so long, I listened to them. I was diagnosed with attention deficit disorder at a young age. I was laughed at, I was talked about, I was picked on and I was humiliated and belittled and this was done by the people that I love and said they loved me. I mean you don't have to go far to define hatred, especially when it's coming from your own family. I think that's the worst kind because they know you intimately. If it was somebody from the street that said the same thing, that probably wouldn't have hurt as much but being that it was coming from inside the house made it hurt that much more. I don't think I can even sit up here and put into words the pain that I carried with me throughout my life from a childhood of belittling. But Just as Mr. Smith learns to overcome adversities, we must learn to do the same. What I never knew is that this defect that everyone picked on me and humiliated me for would be useful when I became a nurse. In my neighborhood, there was no use for my attributes but when you take something that doesn't fit and put it where it belongs, the results are amazing. I didn't belong where I was but when I got into nursing, it all made sense because I can run circles around the average nurse doctor or anybody else who chooses to try to keep up with me. I can work numerous hours and not get tired. I am like an endless ball of energy the majority of the time. It has also been an amazing attribute to have while raising my kids. It has allowed me to play with my kids and have so many great times due to my endless energy and my being a kid at heart. But I said that to let you know that we all have somewhere we belong and you just have to find your place. This world is one big puzzle and I guarantee there's a place you fit. You just have to find that place that God designed just for you and when you get there, enjoy every minute of it because it will be right where you were meant to be. Life gives us all kinds of disadvantages but it is up to each individual to not only master that shortcoming but also fulfill their purpose in life. If you ever get to the point where you feel that your life does not have any meaning or that you cannot make it with the defects or shortcomings you have, I want you to always remember that Mr. Smith didn't give up. I didn't give up. Mr. Williams didn't give up. Mr. Jacobs didn't give up and you are not going to give up either. **I don't care what it takes. You stand up, brush yourself off, you look at yourself in the mirror and you tell yourself, "today, I'm going to be the best me I can be because I'm too great to go to the waist."** I want you to always remember that I'm in your corner and that I'm rooting for you because I know you're going to change the world. I know you are probably reading this like little me with all of my faults to change the world, right? But I say in response, you see this little seed, there is a tree in there. If most looked at it right now they would say it was useless. It might seem impossible that something so great can come from something so small but given enough time, it would reveal without a doubt its greatness for all the world to gaze upon. So never let your shortcomings be your limits. Instead, let nothing stop you from becoming all that you were meant to be because, in the end, the only limit is your mind.

DR. STERLINGZENGER

Dr. Sterlingzinger represented everybody with a dream. The doctor had a dream he believed in and when he told others about it, they laughed at him; they picked on him; they told him how foolish he was to think in such a manner. **I think the most valuable thing that the doctor did was that he had faith in himself in the face of adversity.** You always come up against people who tell you that you can never become what you dream of, that you can never become what you imagine about yourself but I'm here to tell you that if you dream it, you can be it. **Your dreams are only previews of what your life can be if you decide to develop the discipline it takes to get there**. There is nothing in this life that you cannot conquer or that you cannot achieve if you decide that you want it. This doctor reminds me of me. I can relate to so much of this book that it's almost scary when I read it because, in so many different areas, I see myself. But I remember when I first decided to become a nurse; I was working in a factory around a bunch of men and I remember I got laughed at, picked on, and ridiculed because I wanted to be a male nurse. Although they laughed at me and joked repeatedly, I continued with my dream because I knew I wanted to be a nurse. I graduated and I have been working as a nurse for the past 9 years. In these past nine years, one thing that I can say is for sure is that I'm so glad I did not listen to the masses because all of those men who laughed, ridiculed, and picked on me are still in the same spot working the same machines in the same filthy factory and I must admit I am doing all right for myself. If the doctor would have given up on his techniques and his invention, then so many more people would have lost their lives needlessly due to a few men and their archaic thinking. I'm so glad he continued to dream even when everyone including his family didn't believe in him or his invention. Life is only going to be what you make it, so if you're going to dream, why not dare to dream big.

This book is something that I am proud of and I hope that it speaks to you the same way it has spoken to me. I am so grateful to be able to write this for you. I hope that it is what you need to help set you on the right track so you can take off and never look back. You are so much more than all of your circumstances and shortcomings. I pray you become all that you can dream up. Take care of yourself and be great because greatness is who you truly are if you believe.

THE END

P.S I would love to hear from you so please feel free to write a comment as I read them all. I would love to know how my work speaks to you and hopefully helps you change your life for the better. Don't forget to rate my book as it will help me in my dream to reach many people around the world. Will you help me do this? Thanks so much in advance and may many heaps of blessings fall on your head forevermore.

EMAIL ME

www.harrisduane36@gmail.com